THEN AND THERE SERIES
GENERAL EDITOR
MARJORIE REEVES

Merchant Adventurers in the East

ANNE LONSDALE

Illustrated from contemporary sources

LONGMAN

LONGMAN GROUP LIMITED
London
*Associated companies, branches and representatives
throughout the world*

© Longman Group Ltd 1980

First published 1980
ISBN 0 582 21723 7

Set in 11/12½pt Baskerville, Monophoto 169

Printed in Hong Kong by
Wilture Enterprises (International) Ltd.

Contents

To the Reader

Nowadays the world is a very small place. Men have landed on the moon and we are used to pictures of astronauts crossing its dusty surface. This book is about a time when China and India seemed more remote from Europe than the moon does today. A few daring travellers had made their way across the mountains and deserts of Central Asia and had written accounts of what they found. They brought back spices, silks, *porcelain*, precious stones and pearls. But ordinary people still did not know which of these travellers' tales to believe. Some said that silk grew on the back of a rare kind of sheep, others that in some places men went to war in wooden castles carried on the backs of huge grey creatures called elephants whose noses were as long as serpents. It was hard to tell which of these stories to believe.

In 1340 it was possible to visit India and China or Cathay, as it was often called, but only by land. No one had ever tried to sail south from Africa or west across the Atlantic to reach the East by sea. Most people thought that the world was flat and that any madman who sailed too far south or west would tip over the edge and vanish. In this book we shall see what happened when sailors first dared to travel the long sea-routes to the East.

The discovery of these trade-routes was very different from finding the New World across the Atlantic. For one thing, people in Europe knew that China and India were there. What was needed was a new way to reach them. Then, in the first fifty years, the work was almost all done by one tiny country, Portugal. Only the colony of the Philippines was set up by Spain. For these first years, from the first voyage of Bartholemew Diaz around the Cape of Good Hope, other countries like England and Holland began to follow Portugal's lead. But at first they collected their cargoes more by piracy than by trade.

Another big difference was that the Portuguese came to trade in the great markets of India and the Far East where there were already many foreign merchants, Arabs, Indians, Chinese, Javanese, Malays. They had Arab and Chinese pilots to show them the way. And they found themselves among old and splendid civilisations which they realised were in many ways better than their own at home. So this story is not so much one of particular heroes like Columbus or Magellan but of the courage and daring of thousands of ordinary sailors, chiefly Portuguese, English and Dutch who risked the journey to the East to look for adventures and a fortune. Many came to a watery grave, but some lived to tell of the wonders they had seen. Their stories are in this book. Many of the places mentioned here can be seen in the map on the inside front cover.

Words printed in *italics* are explained in the Glossary on page 93.

1 Genghis Khan and the Land Route to Cathay

Long ago the Romans bought Chinese silks which had been carried by Syrian merchants from the far-away lands of the 'Seres', or Silk People. In the Dark Ages, after the Roman Empire had ended, the secret of silk-making was brought to the court of the *Byzantine* emperors and silk was woven in Europe. But the Silk Road from China was dangerous and few dared travel it.

In AD 1200 things began to change. First Genghis Khan became ruler of all the Mongol peoples in Central Asia. His *nomad* soldiers, mounted on little Mongol ponies, carried all their supplies with them on their backs or slung from their ponies' saddles, so that they could easily outstrip the armies of city-dwelling people. Genghis captured the great cities of the Silk Road, Samarkand and Bokhara; he even reached the borders of China in the east and Turkey in the west. His son and grandson, Ogodai Khan and Kubilai Khan completed his conquests and Kubilai became the Emperor of China from 1260 to 1295. These Mongol conquests weakened the power of the *Moslem* peoples who ruled the Mediterranean coasts of Asia, the countries we know as Syria, Lebanon and Turkey. For years the Christians of Europe had been fighting against the Moslems of the Middle East to win back the Holy Land, and above all, the Holy City of Jerusalem. (You can read about these wars in another Then and There called 'The Crusades'.) Now, at last, they saw that the way east was not

Opposite: *The Roman view of the world: a medieval copy of a map by Ptolemy, a famous Roman geographer. Britain, South East Asia and Africa are all on the edges of the world*

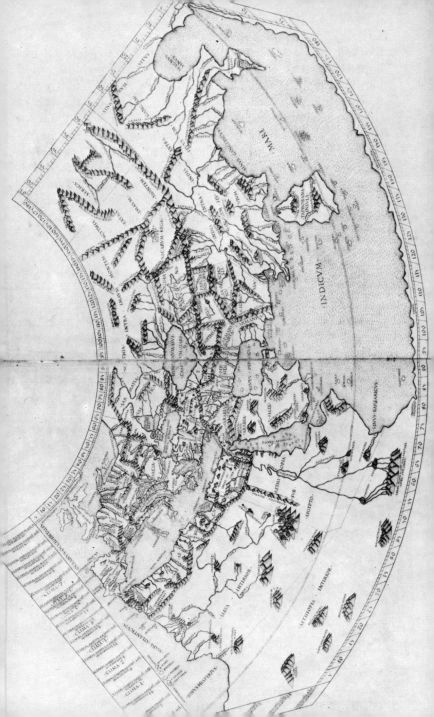

blocked by the Moslems. As the Mongols were *pagans*, it was hoped that they could be made into Christians and would join in a Holy War against the Moslem rulers. That is why the first travellers who ventured into Asia after the rise of Genghis Khan were monks and friars, like William of Ruysbruck and John of Plano Carpini. They made few *converts* among the people they called 'Tartars', but they returned to tell of what they had seen. Their accounts of the great peace and good order which they found in Asia encouraged merchants to follow them, and for the next hundred years they came and went with their goods from Europe to China with more ease and freedom than they would enjoy if they travelled the same route today.

Marco Polo leaves Venice. The four bronze horses in St Mark's Square are in the top left corner

The best known of these travellers was Marco Polo. You will find the full story of his journey to China and the posts he held under the Great Khan, Kubilai, in another Then and There called 'Marco Polo and Cathay'. When he returned to Italy and wrote the story of his travels, many people refused to believe him. But within fifty years, by AD 1340, travelling to China had become quite common and European merchants knew the cities of the Silk Road and the routes south to India quite well. Their customers at home relied on the spices they imported and enjoyed luxuries like silk, precious stones and pearls.

One of these merchants was Francisco Balduccci Pegolotti. In 1340 he wrote an account of the eastern trade in his 'Book of the Descriptions of Countries'. He described the taxes and customs dues and the different weights, measures and coinages in use along the route to the East. Here is his advice on Chinese paper money:

> Whatever silver the merchants carry with them as far as Cathay, the Lord of Cathay [Kubilai Khan] will take from them and put into his treasury. And to merchants who thus bring silver they give that paper money of theirs in exchange. This is of yellow paper stamped with the seal of the Lord Kubilai Khan. And with the money you can readily buy silk and all other merchandise that you have a desire to buy. And all the people of the country are bound to receive it.

As for customs dues, 'At Tana [on the Sea of Azov],' he wrote, 'on wine and ox-hides and tails and horse-hides the Genoese and Venetians pay four per cent, and all other peoples five per cent, while gold, silver and pearls pay no duties.' Pegolotti also compared the different weights by which goods were sold, giving us a vivid picture of what was to be found in the markets of central Asia:

> Wax, iron, tin, copper, pepper, ginger, all coarser spices, cotton, *madder*, and sweet cheese, flax and oil, honey and the like sell by the *Great Pound*.

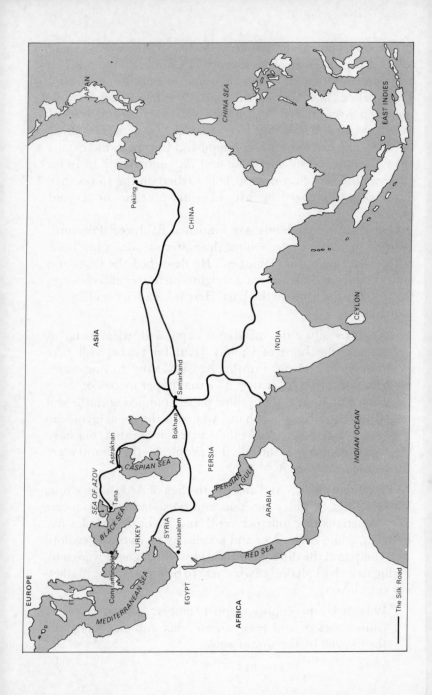

Silk, saffron, amber wrought in rosaries and the like and all small spices sell by the *Little Pound*.

Foxes, sables, martens, wolf skins, deer skins and all cloths of silk or gold sell by the piece.

Tails sell by the bundle at twenty to the bundle. Caviar is sold by the fusco and the fusco is the tail half of a fish's skin full of fish's roe.

Pegolotti added: 'Do not forget that if you treat the customs-house officers with respect and make them something of a present in goods or money as well as their clerks and interpreters they will behave with great politeness and always be ready to tax your wares with a very low value.'

Pegolotti also described 'Things Needful for Merchants Who Desire to Make the Journey to Cathay':

In the first place, you must let your beard grow long. At Tana you should hire an interpreter. And you must not try to save money by taking a bad one instead of a good one. For the extra wages of a good one will not cost you so much as you will save by having him . . . and from Tana travelling to Astrakhan you should take with you twenty-five days' provisions, that is to say, flour and salt, fish, for as to meat, you will find enough of it at all the places along the road. . . . The road you travel from Tana to Cathay is perfectly safe whether by day or night, according to what the merchants say who have used it. . . . Cathay is a province which contains a multitude of cities and towns. Among these there is one, the capital city, in which there is a vast amount of trade, called Cambalec [Peking]. The said city has a circuit of a hundred miles [160 kilometres] around the walls and is all full of people and houses and of dwellers in the said city.

You may calculate that a merchant with interpreter and two men servants and goods worth twenty-five thousand golden florins [about £12,500] could spend on his way to Cathay from sixty to eighty somni of silver, if he manage well; and for the road back again, including all charges, the costs will be about five somni per head of pack animals. And you may reckon the somno to be worth five gold florins.

(A florin was worth about fifty pence today so that the value of the goods was over £12,000, the cost of the journey estimated at £150 to £200 and of the journey back about £12 per pack animal.)

Pegolotti concluded, 'Even when the road is at its worst, if you are some sixty men together you will go as safely as if you were in your own house.' If the Silk Road had remained as safe as this, merchants could have continued to rely on Pegolotti's advice and would have had no need for a new route to Cathay. Years might have passed before anyone set out across the Atlantic and discovered a new continent in the West. But, as quickly as it had been established, the Great Peace of Genghis Khan was destroyed. A new leader arose among the nomads of Central Asia, called Timur the Lame, because of a crippling wound he suffered in battle when he was young. In the West he was known as Tamburlane, and although he died in 1405 his name could still cause so much terror over 150 years later that an Elizabethan playwright, Christopher Marlowe, wrote two plays about him and his deeds.

Tamburlane was a great conqueror, known as the '*Scourge* of God', but he did not leave behind a strong new empire. Instead the old empire split into small cities and states. In China, the Chinese drove the Mongols out and a Chinese Emperor ruled once more. The foreigners who had served the hated Mongol rulers were no longer welcome. In central Asia, Tamburlane made his capital at Samarkand. Although he had such a terrible reputation, he eagerly collected books and works of art and was particularly fond of gardens. His descendants, the Moghul emperors, enjoyed the same things. We shall meet them 200 years later, ruling in India. Further west, the Turks, who had been held back by the Mongol Empire,

Mongol encampment. Mongols are cooking, eating, or resting against their saddles. In the right hand corner are the weapons and supplies they carried with them on horseback

began fresh conquests of their own. In 1453 the great capital of Constantinople or Byzantium fell into Turkish hands. Trade overland between Christian merchants and the East became impossible, for the Turks were Moslems and sworn enemies of all Christians.

The experience of men like Pegolotti was useless now but people in Europe had come to depend on the goods these men brought from the East, especially spices from the Indies. In those days, farmers had to slaughter most of their cattle, sheep and pigs in the autumn as it was not possible to feed them through the winter. So for six months of the year everyone lived on salted, and often bad, meat. Spices like pepper were a wonderful way of hiding the taste of bad food and adding variety to fresh foods like oatmeal porridge and root vegetables which were rather boring and monotonous. The growing demand for these spices led merchant adventurers to risk their lives sailing south and west into the Atlantic for a new route to the Indies.

13

2　Prince Henry the Navigator

Merchants and sailors from the great ports of Venice and Genoa in Italy had played a large part in the opening of trade with the East. (Marco Polo was himself a Venetian.) They now suffered from a drop in profits as they had to buy spices from Moslem traders in Syria and Egypt who charged high prices. But they had learned more than other Europeans from travellers to the East. So the more adventurous among them began to look for new ways of reaching the Indies. Many of the explorers to the East and the West in the century ahead were to come from these Italian ports, including Christopher Columbus. Meanwhile, they began to keep records and maps called 'Portolani', showing currents, shoals and prevailing winds which were the forerunners of our modern charts. They also experimented with discoveries like the *mariners' compass*, a Chinese invention which had recently been brought to the West.

Italian seamen were the first to decide to try new routes to the Indies, but it was to be in Portugal that they found the practical help needed to make their voyages possible. Portugal was a small, rather poor country when the first great voyagers of exploration set sail, but at the beginning of the fifteenth century there were special reasons why she could think about such adventures and wanted to expand her power overseas. For centuries, Spain and Portugal had been ruled by a Moslem race, the *Moors*, who had originally crossed over to Europe from North Africa. Spain did not win back the last Moorish stronghold in the south, around the city of Granada, until 1492. But Portugal had defeated her Moorish rulers for good and driven them from her soil in 1249. Portuguese troops had even

A map-maker at work. He has magnetised the compass needle on the corner of his desk with a lodestone floating in a large bowl of mercury on the floor. He is probably transferring the instructions from a log-book under his left hand to a chart

chased the Moors back into Africa across the Straits of Gibraltar and defeated them there, at the Battle of Ceuta in 1415, the same year in which the English defeated the French at the Battle of Agincourt.

When one country conquers another and rules over it by force it is hardly surprising if the original inhabitants hate their conquerors. The Portuguese hated their Moorish rulers with particular ferocity because they were Christians and the Moors were Moslems who had also captured the Holy City of Jerusalem and prevented Christians from worshipping there. Many Portuguese believed quite sincerely that when they killed an 'infidel' or 'unbeliever' as they called the Moors, they were doing the work of God. An English historian, Friar Thomas of Walsingham, described the Battle of Ceuta and Portugal's defeat of the Moors as well as the life of Prince Henry the Navigator who had fought there himself:

The King of Portugal overcame the Moors, many thousands of them being sent to hell, and took their city called Ceuta . . . Henry, having given proofs of his bravery against the infidels at Ceuta, planned how he might advance the honour of his name in conquests which others had not yet attempted and discovery of countries yet unknown. To this end he spent his life, unmarried, in the study of mathematics. He chose the clear air of Cape St. Vincent, that he might better put into practice his mathematical theory, in instruments and their use, in sending out ships at his own expense to discover remoter parts; of which he had heard both by enquiry of captives taken at Ceuta and guessed at by his own study and reason, that the Atlantic and Indian Oceans were connected, the one leading to the other or, rather, being one continuous ocean.

Thomas Walsingham thought that Prince Henry's expeditions were sent out to defeat the Moors and convert new Christians. Another reason why Christians were eager to explore the East was the old story of Prester John. There were rumours of a great Christian empire somewhere in the East, ruled by an emperor called Prester John (his first name comes from the Greek word Presbyter, which means Priest). The Christian monarchs in Europe hoped that he would join them in their unending wars against the 'infidels'. Now Prince Henry sent out explorers by land as well as sea to look for him. But it was not until 1491, some years after Prince Henry's death, that Pedro de Covilhan, an ambassador from King John II of Portugal, reached Ethiopia in Africa and found there the mysterious Christian empire he had been seeking. Unfortunately, the emperor, though rich and powerful, did not want travellers from the outside world and would not join in a Holy War against the Moors.

So there were three reasons for Prince Henry's explorations to defeat the Moors, to look for new Christian allies and to search for the spice markets of India and Cathay. The north-west coast of Africa was barren, desert country where only a few tribes lived by fishing. But the islands off the African coast and out in the Atlantic were fertile and provided useful harbours for ships to take on water and supplies on their journeys south (see the map on page 22). Portugal began to do a brisk trade in sugar which she grew on the island of Madeira and in corn from the Azores. By the time of Prince Henry's death in 1460 the Portuguese had also set up a thriving colony in the Cape Verde Islands, but it was above all the trade in

A Portuguese portrait of Prince Henry the Navigator at Cape St Vincent

gold and slaves found further south along the west coast of Africa which gave Prince Henry the money to equip his fleets of explorers and persuade the people of Portugal and adventurers from abroad to join him.

At first the sailors were afraid. Samuel Purchas (you can read about him in the How Do We Know? section) described Prince Henry's difficulties: 'Twelve years had passed since the prince began this enterprise before Cape Bojador could be   17 passed; such was the common belief in stormy seas, strong currents, whirlpools which could swallow ships beyond that cape.' By 1441, however, the explorers had reached the part of West Africa now called Sierra Leone. Here, 'they traded with the Negroes for exchange of their men (native prisoners captured further up the coast) for which they received gold and other slaves, so that they called the place Rio d'Oro, or Golden River...gold made everyone take back their former complaints and now the prince was praised.'

Once men realised that voyages of discovery were profitable as well as dangerous, Prince Henry found sailors for his ships. A young Venetian, Luigi Cadamosto, tells us how he enlisted for one of the Prince's voyages, in 1455. He was travelling along the coast of Portugal when he met one of Prince Henry's secretaries, who told him that Prince Henry permitted any who wished to sail under one of two conditions:

1. He might fit out the ship at his own expense and load her with merchandise—on his return he had to pay one quarter of all he brought back, keeping three-quarters for himself, or 2. Prince Henry would equip a ship for whoever wished to go if he provided the cargo. On return all that had been brought back from those parts would be halved and if nothing had been brought then Prince Henry would pay the expense. If any wished to go the Prince would receive him gladly for he believed that in those parts they would find spices and other valuable products and he knew that the Venetians were more skilled in these affairs than any other nation. I definitely made up my mind to go for I was young, well-fitted to sustain all hardships, desirous of seeing the world and things never seen before by our nation and I hoped also to draw from it honour and profit.

Cadamosto went on a voyage for Prince Henry and lived to tell of his journey down the west coast of Africa:

At first the coast is sandy. There are many shoals of sand and rock and strong currents so that one only sails by day

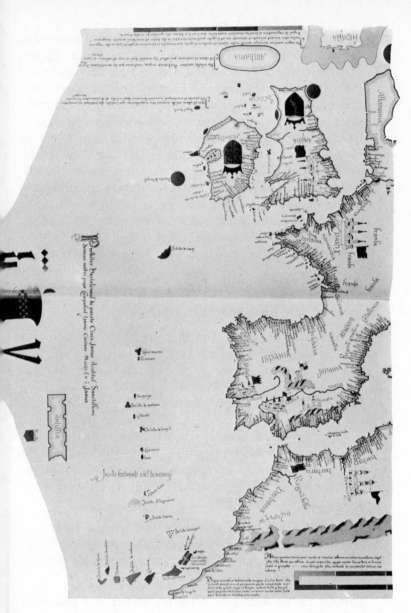

This map of 1455 shows Europe, part of the African coast and an island in the Atlantic, the first chart of the discovery of America

with the *lead* in hand (to take soundings) and according to the state of the tide. The people here have many camels on which they carry brass and silver for Barbary and other things to Timbucto and the Land of the Blacks. Thence they carry away pepper and gold. In these sandy districts there are many lions, leopards and ostriches, the eggs of which I have often eaten and found good. The people wear their hair down to their shoulders—the hair is black and anointed every day with fish oil so that it smells strongly, which they consider very fine. Our ships were strange to them—some believe they were great sea-birds with white wings flying and when the sails were lowered for landing, that they were fishes. Others said that they were phantoms that went by night, at which they were greatly terrified.

Cadamosto was one of the first travellers to describe what happens when you cross the Equator, although some of the effects were more imaginary than real:

On the Equator, it is so hot, they say, that the blood goes bad. So the natives mix salt in a little jar with water and drink it every day—they say that this saves them. We saw the pole star once only when it appeared very low down over the sea, about a third of a lance above the horizon. In the morning, when day breaks, there is no dawn at the rising of the sun, as in our parts, where between dawn and sunrise there is a short interval before the shadows of night disappear; the sun appears suddenly though it is not bright for the space of half an hour as the sun is dull, as it were, and smokey on first rising.

Cadamosto reached the mouth of the Senegal river and found settled and prosperous villages and markets unlike the barren coasts of the Sahara. Here the sailors were able to trade as well as explore:

The natives brought cotton clothes and thread woven in their fashion, some white, others white with blue stripes or
20   red, white and blue, excellently made. They also brought

The Portuguese
used caravels
like this
to explore the
coast of Africa

many apes and baboons of various species, large and small,
of which there were very large numbers in these parts.
These they bartered for objects of very little worth. [The
Africans were amazed at Cadamosto's appearance]...
They crowded round to see me as though I were a marvel. It
seemed to be a new experience to them to see Christians.
They marvelled no less at my clothing than at my white
skin. My clothes were after the Spanish fashion, a doublet
of black damask with a short cloak of grey wool over it.
They examined the woollen cloth with much amazement.
Some touched my hands and limbs and rubbed them with
spit to discover whether my whiteness was a dye or flesh.
Finding it was flesh, they were astonished. The women of
this country are very pleasant and light-hearted, ready to
sing and dance, especially the young girls. They dance,
however, only at night by the light of the moon. Their
dances are very different from ours.

In 1456, Diogo Gomez made a further voyage down the
coast of Africa for Prince Henry, as far as the mouth of the river

Gambia. But this was to be the last voyage that the Prince sent out from his home at Cape Vincent. Samuel Purchas considered him a model explorer:

> Prince Henry never gave up his endeavours of discovery until he died 43 years after Madeira had been discovered. In all which time his ships travelled no further than from Cape Bojador to Sierra Leone, 1,110 miles [1,800 kilometres] space in almost fifty years continuous cares and costs.

Prince Henry and Bartholemew Diaz explore the African coast

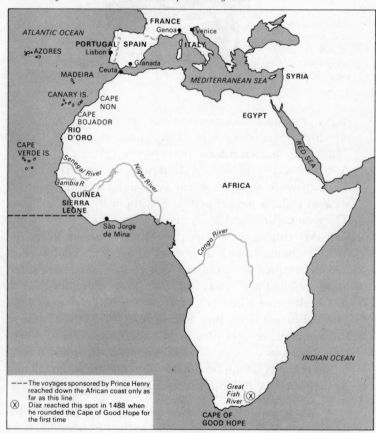

--- The voyages sponsored by Prince Henry reached down the African coast only as far as this line

ⓧ Diaz reached this spot in 1488 when he rounded the Cape of Good Hope for the first time

3　The Voyage of Vasco da Gama

Prince Henry had collected a great deal of valuable knowledge. The rocks and shoals off the African coast had all been recorded on charts. But perhaps the most important discovery was the rich trade in gold and slaves.

King John of Portugal, who succeeded to the throne in 1481, also encouraged explorers. The Equator had first been crossed in 1471, ten years earlier. In this chapter we shall see how the Portuguese, led by Vasco da Gama, at last found the new sea-route to the Indies round the Cape of Good Hope.

By December 1485 King John was confident that his sailors would soon reach the Indian Ocean and meet Prester John and other Christian monarchs there. In 1486, as Purchas tells us, Bartholomew Diaz became the first man to sail around the southern tip of Africa:

> King John sent both by land and by sea to enquire of the Indies and of the great emperor Prester John; by sea two *pinnaces* of fifty tons each under the command of Bartholomew Diaz, with a little supply ship, in August 1486. Diaz set certain negroes ashore in different places who had before been brought to Portugal and well-treated so that among these savages they might tell how great and how civilised the Portuguese were and to make known his desire to find ways of meeting Prester John. He gave names to places discovered, and erected pillars or crosses of stone. But his people, very uneasy, urged him to return, saying their supplies were finished and the supply ship was lost. But he went on so far that he first discovered the famous

Vasco da Gama

Cape, which because of his many troubles, he called Capo Tormentoso, or the Tempestuous Cape: but King John, hoping thereby to discover the Indies, named it on his return the Cape of Good Hope. He returned in December 1487, 16 months and 17 days after his setting out, having discovered 10,050 miles [16,180 kilometres] of coast. He found on his way back his supply ship, wherein he had left 9 men of which only 3 were left alive; of which one, Fernand Colazzo, died with sudden joy at their sight.

So in 1487 it was proved once and for all that it was possible to sail round the southern tip of Africa. But the sea beyond the Cape of Good Hope was still unknown and unexplored and several years were to pass before the next voyage to the East. In 1495 King John fell ill and died. His successor, King Manuel, soon began preparations for a new voyage. Bartholomew Diaz was set to build ships better suited to a long voyage than his small *Caravels* with *lateen sails* had been. The new ships were bigger and heavier, *square-rigged* ships called 'Naus' in Portuguese. (You can read all about ships at this time in another Then and There called 'The Elizabethan Ship'.)

The new captain for this voyage was a nobleman, Vasco da
24 Gama. Whilst Diaz was preparing his ships, da Gama trained

his crews. He encouraged his sailors to learn a trade, as carpenters, rope-makers, *caulkers*, blacksmiths or plank-makers and 'gave them an increase of two *crusados* a month beyond the sailor's pay of five crusados a month; so that all rejoiced at learning so as to draw more pay.' His voyage was well prepared in other ways too—strict rules and punishments were laid down for sailors and officers alike. The ships were laden with small presents such as glass beads and bells for trading with the natives along the coast of Africa, for Diaz had found such things useful on his journey. They also carried large stores of food, for Diaz had discovered that for several weeks at a time near the Cape of Good Hope ships were far from villages where fresh water and fresh food could be obtained. Poor diet made the sailors sick and discontented. So each man was to have one and a half pounds of biscuits, one pound of beef or half a pound of pork, two and a half pints of fresh water, one and a quarter pints of wine and a small quantity of oil and vinegar daily. On *fast days* he would receive half a pound of rice and some dried fish or cheese instead. The ships also carried flour, lentils, sardines, plums, almonds, garlic, mustard, salt, sugar and honey to add variety. But this careful planning in advance did not prevent da Gama's sailors from suffering from *scurvy*, a disease which later sailors suffered from a great deal on the long voyages across the Pacific Ocean, but which up to this time had not troubled them because ships rarely sailed far from the sight of land and could put in regularly for fresh water, fruit and vegetables.

When his preparations were complete, Vasco da Gama set sail down the river Tagus from Lisbon on 9 July 1497. When at last the fleet reached the Cape of Good Hope his men were dissatisfied:

they were impatient to turn back...He gave them great encouragement without ever sleeping or taking rest, but always taking part with them in hardships, coming up at the *bosun's pipe* as they all did. As the days were very short it always seemed night. At night the ships showed lights to each other so as not to part company. Seeing how much they had travelled and did not reach land they sailed in a wider circle so as to make it and because they did not find it (because they were looking on the wrong side) and the wind and sea were moderate, they knew that they had rounded the Cape, on which great joy fell upon them.

The first land round the Cape had no inhabitants at all; almost at once, they ran into storms and their supplies were very low. Again, they wished to turn back, but da Gama insisted that they should remember 'they had already doubled the Cape of Storms [the old name of the Cape of Good Hope] and were in that region they had come to seek, to discover India. On accomplishing which, and returning to Portugal, they would gain such great honour and reward from the King of Portugal for their children.'

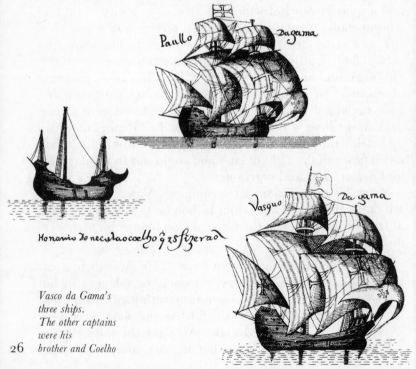

Vasco da Gama's
three ships.
The other captains
were his
brother and Coelho

After the rough weather it was necessary to repair the ships and here Diaz's careful preparations of the ships were to prove valuable. They broke up one of the ships and removed its rudder, 'because the ships had all been built to the same pattern and size so that all might be able to take advantage of any part of them. Then they burned the ship in order to recover the nails which were in great quantity and a great advantage for other difficulties they met with later.' No doubt the crew also found itself work to do on other ships, for many sailors were already sick with scurvy, 'their feet and their hands swelling and their gums growing over their teeth so that they could not eat.' It must have been a relief to these weary men to anchor near villages with fresh supplies and welcome their first visitors:

Some blacks came aboard without any fear and sat them-selves down as if they were old acquaintances. No-one knew how to speak with them. Then they gave them biscuits and cake and slices of bread with marmalade: this they did not understand until they saw our people eat and then they ate it and as they liked the taste, they ate in a great hurry and would not share with one another.

The sailors were now almost at the end of their voyage of exploration. Soon they came upon a little fleet of seven native boats. A young man in dirty Arab dress spoke to them in Arabic and told them to sail north to Sofala where Arab traders and pilots would guide them to India. Passing Sofala by mistake, they came to port in Mozambique. Here they met for the first time the hatred which Moorish kings showed to Christian traders who suddenly appeared in their ports. Both in Mozambique and their next port of call, Mombasa, the rulers tried to wreck Portuguese ships by piloting them on to shoals, or to overpower the men by sending aboard large parties of 'friendly ambassadors' whom the Portuguese quickly learned not to trust. Vasco da Gama behaved towards them with the cold cruelty he always showed to Moslems who crossed his path.

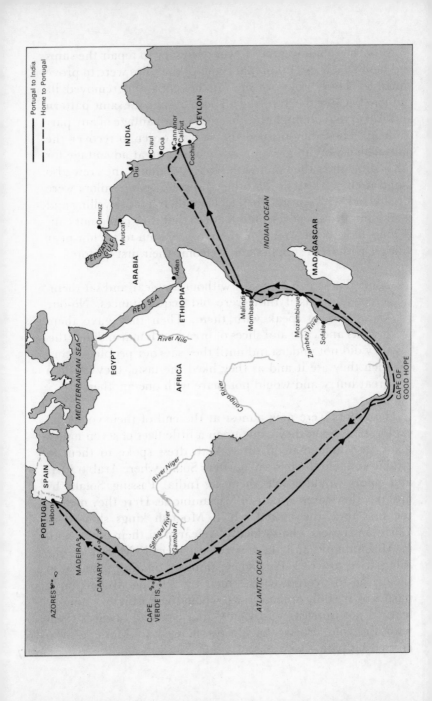

At noon he questioned two Moors whom we had on board by dropping boiling oil on their skins so that they might confess any treachery intended against us and when this torture was being applied a second time one of the Moors, although he had his hands tied behind him, threw himself into the sea, whilst the other did so during the morning watch. Swimmers then came to cut the cables and the rigging and these and other wicked tricks were played on us by these dogs, but our Lord did not allow them to succeed because they were Unbelievers.

From Mombasa the fleet sailed to Malindi on the coast of Africa just south of the Equator. Their worst adventures were over.

The town lies in a bay and it extends along the shore. Its houses are lofty and well whitewashed and have many windows; on the land side are palm groves and all around it maize and vegetables are being cultivated. We remained in this town nine days and had fêtes, sham fights and musical performances. Here we first met with people they called Indian Christians.

For several years to come, the Portuguese did not realise that those Indians who were not Moslems were *Hindus*. They had all heard of St. Thomas, one of the disciples of Jesus who travelled to India and of the Church he founded there. They knew nothing of the great religions of Hinduism and Buddhism and there were enough likenesses between the beliefs and forms of worship of Hinduism and Christianity to confuse them even when they stood inside Hindu temples at Hindu ceremonies. The Hindu sailors of Malindi were shown an altar piece of the Virgin and Jesus from on board ship.

When they saw the picture they prostrated themselves and they came to say their prayers in front of it bringing offerings of clothes and pepper and other things. The Indians are little brown men; they wear little clothing and have long beards and long hair which they braid. They told us that they ate no beef. Their language differs from that of the Arabs but some of them know a little of it as they do much trade with them.

The king of Malindi received Vasco da Gama with great kindness and told him to sail to Calicut on the south-west coast of India 'which is the country where the pepper and ginger grows'. He gave the Portuguese experienced and friendly pilots for the rest of the voyage. So in some ways the period of exploration into the unknown came to an end at the port of Malindi. Many ports in the Far East had never been visited by European travellers before, but Marco Polo had visited some on his voyage home to India from China. Nevertheless, many surprises and dangers still awaited them as Samuel Purchas tells us, describing the triumphant arrival of Vasco da Gama in India:

> 19 May 1498, they had sight of land, being the high mountains near to Calicut, and came within two miles [three kilometres] of the city the same day. He gave thanks to God and set one of his prisoners ashore [ten had sailed with him on condition that they would be given their freedom if they acted as scouts in particularly dangerous situations]; he was almost crushed by the crowds pressing to see a man of such strange appearance, till at last two merchants from Tunis recognized him to be a Spaniard. One of them asked him in Spanish, 'The devil take you, what has brought you hither?' They invited him home and having made him eat and drink went on board with him to da Gama and offered him all kindness; telling him that the king of Calicut would be glad of their coming.'

It seems strange that after such a long voyage into unknown seas the expedition should be met in such a way. But it must have been a great relief to the Portuguese prisoner alone in the

Opposite: *A mid-sixteenth-century map of the Indian Ocean. Can you find Aden on the Arabian Gulf; the Persian Gulf and Calicut? Calicut is on the south-west side of India opposite a deep inlet*

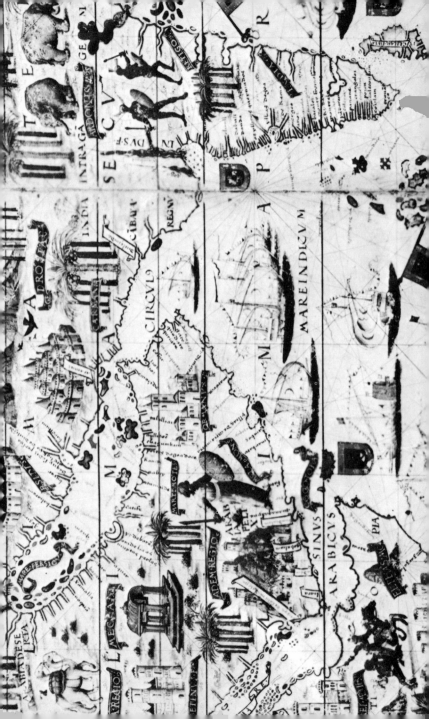

Indian crowd to hear a language that he could understand and receive a friendly greeting. The two merchants from Tunis arranged for members of da Gama's crew to be sent to the king of Calicut as messengers. Da Gama soon followed them himself to pay his respects, leaving his brother, Paulo da Gama, in charge of the fleet. He also left strict instructions that if anything happened to him, Paulo was to sail back to Portugal at once, for two little ships and their crews could do nothing to save their friends on shore if trouble broke out.

The embassy led by Vasco da Gama then set out carried in *litters* sent specially for them by the king. Here is Samuel Purchas' account of their arrival in the king's palace.

> It was a large hall with many benches built up one above the other like a theatre. The floor was covered with silk and the walls hung with curtains of silk embroidered with gold. The king lay on a rich bed with a turban on his head set with stones and decorated with gold, clothed in silk and having many gold buckles on his breast. On his ears hung jewels of great value; his toes and fingers, covered with rings and gems, made a glorious sight. He was tall and handsome and his presence was full of majesty. Da Gama greeted him with a bow as he would have greeted the king of Portugal and was seated next to him whilst the other Portuguese sat down nearby. Water was brought to wash and cool their hands and various fruits to refresh them.

The king asked them why they had come and Vasco da Gama delivered letters to him from the king of Portugal. The Indian ruler agreed to regard this distant European king as a brother and gave da Gama a house in his city and the embassy was taken there to rest. They noticed that the city was large, the houses set in their own gardens and orchards but not very handsomely built; for only the king's palace could be built of stone. At first the embassy seemed to be going well, even the sailors enjoyed themselves; 'as to us others we amused ourselves singing and dancing to the sounds of trumpets and enjoyed ourselves much.' But trouble soon spoiled this happy meeting, for the Moslem traders of Calicut were unwilling to see these Portuguese rivals in their markets. A Portuguese historian commented, 'here they had their principal port for fishing, pepper and drugs, which they transported to Mecca and spread over Turkey and thence to all the provinces of Christendom so the Moors could see the great inconvenience which would fall on them and their trade if the Portuguese should establish trade in Calicut.' The Portuguese had permission to load a small cargo which might be only the first of many. So the Moslem traders and city officials ordered da Gama to leave without it, taking seven of his men as hostages. In return, da Gama seized twenty fishermen and made as if to set sail at once, with cargo and prisoners still aboard. At that the hostages were hurriedly returned and da Gama released most of his fishermen, though a few wretched Indians were taken to Portugal and shown to King Manuel as a curiosity. He set sail at once and was attacked by over sixty small ships; the skill of his seamen and the power of his guns allowed him to escape unharmed.

It was a hard voyage. Da Gama had Moorish pilots with him who steered a straight course and there were no terrible storms at the Cape. But Paulo da Gama fell ill and died in the Canary Islands, almost within sight of Portugal. 'All the crews were sick and the ships could hardly keep afloat, even when the sailors manned the pumps, they were so old that it was a wonder that they kept above water . . . and of the four ships and one hundred men that set out only two ships and fifty-five men returned and these very feeble.' Vasco da Gama was very much upset by his brother's death and did not return with the first ship to Lisbon. But when his first grief was passed he prepared for the short journey from the Canary Islands to Portugal for a hero's welcome. After fifty years of patient effort by Prince Henry and his successors, Portugal had found the new route to the East. The voyage might not have brought Vasco da Gama himself all the happiness for which he must have hoped, but it was to be the beginning of a great empire in the East for Portugal which lasted until this century. 33

4   Empires in India

The Portuguese sent several trading expeditions to India when they knew that Vasco da Gama had been successful. Among them was the expedition led by Pedro Cabral in 1500 which discovered Brazil. On its way to the Cape of Good Hope it sailed right across the Atlantic by accident and claimed the land it found there for Portugal. In 1494 Spain and Portugal had made a treaty called the Treaty of Tordesillas. They agreed that Spain would have all the new lands discovered west of a line drawn north-south 370 leagues west of the Azores islands. But Brazil jutted out so far into the Atlantic that it was in Portugal's half of the world.

Vasco da Gama himself made a second voyage to India in 1502, with a navy of twenty-five ships. His aim was to punish the people of Calicut for allowing Moslem merchants to trade there. He captured fishermen and traders in the harbour and had them hanged, drawn and quartered and sent ashore in an open boat. He then loaded a fine cargo in the two Hindu ports of Cochin and 'Cannanor further down the coast and came home well pleased with his bloodthirsty voyage. Portuguese merchants who had invested in his fleet made a profit of 150 per cent.

The work of setting up a Portuguese empire in the East began in 1508 when the first Viceroy of India, Dom Francisco d'Almeida, arrived in Goa. He believed that the Portuguese must control the sea and not try to conquer an empire on land as well. 'Build no more fortresses than may be absolutely necessary to protect your *factories* from a sudden raid,' he said, 'we can spare no men from the navy.'

For Portugal is a small country. There were not enough able-bodied men to sail the ships, let alone to patrol an empire. Untrained sailors served in Almeida's ships. The story goes that they did not know left from right, let alone port from starboard. So the captain hung up a bunch of onions on one side of the ship and a bunch of garlic on the other. Then the orders rang out, 'Onion your helm' or 'Garlic your helm', and all was well!

Affonso d'Albuquerque,
Viceroy of India
from 1509 to 1515

Under Almeida the Portuguese won a great sea victory against the Egyptian fleet in 1508. From this time there was no one who could stand up to their ships in the Indian Ocean until the arrival of the English and Dutch fleets at the end of the sixteenth century. Under the next Viceroy, Dom Affonso d'Albuquerque, the Portuguese began to fight for power on land as well. Albuquerque, perhaps the finest governor Portuguese India ever had, soon saw that Portugal must hold four key points if she was to keep the power she had won. These were the straits of Malacca (the eastern end of the Indian Ocean) and Ormuz and Aden (the western entrances) as well

35

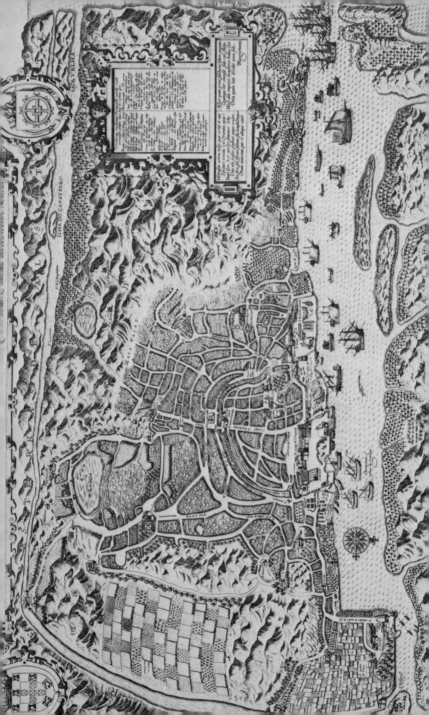

as a land-base in India itself, where the Portuguese fleet could refit and a permanent factory and garrison could be set up. For this, he chose Goa, an easily-defended port on an island separated from the mainland of India by two river-channels filled with crocodiles by an earlier Indian ruler. As he wrote to King Manuel in Portugal:

> In Cochin you cannot cut a stick without asking leave of the Raja. If one of our men refuses to pay full market price in the *Bazaar*, the fort is besieged. In Cochin 500 extra men mean famine...In Goa beef, fish, bread and vegetables are plentiful and an additional 2,000 men are scarcely noticed; in Goa there are gunsmiths, armourers, carpenters, ship-wrights, everything we require.

The Portuguese took Goa in November 1510 and Albuquerque at once proceeded with the next part of his master-plan. He captured the port of Malacca in August 1511. In 1513 he attacked Aden, but here, for the first time, he was unsuccessful. However in 1515 he took the port of Ormuz but fell ill on his way back to Goa and dictated his last letter to King Manuel:

> I leave India with the principal rulers fallen into your power; everything is settled except that it were well to lock the doors of the straits [to capture the port of Aden]. And so I have done what you commanded me. Sire, it were well, if you want to keep India always safe, to continue to make it pay for its own expenses. I pray that as my reward you will remember all this and make my son a nobleman and pay him in full for all his services.

Other Viceroys followed Albuquerque, including the aged Vasco da Gama himself in 1524. The Viceroy became a very powerful man. As Albuquerque himself said, 'Portugal is a very small country. Can Portugal offer me any task equal to one-sixth of what the Viceroy of India has to do?' He had the power of life and death over the army, navy and civil servants

Opposite: *Goa, showing the river where the crocodiles were. There is still room for fields and gardens but later it became crowded*

as well as the citizens of Goa. There were two councils under him, the Council of State and the Council of the Three Estates. When the Portuguese controlled the whole of the Indian Ocean, by 1540, there were five Captains of the five chief Portuguese cities, Mozambique (on the east coast of Africa), Ormuz, Muskat (on the Persian Gulf) Ceylon (Sri Lanka) and Malacca, all under the Viceroy's control.

One of Albuquerque's most important rules for his subjects, which was followed later in all of Portugal's colonies, was that Portuguese who came to India should marry Indian wives and bring up their families there. Their children would have all the privileges of Portuguese citizens. For Portugal itself could not provide the men to run an empire—it had barely enough for its navy. In this way, as in others, like paying for their own troops, the colonies had to 'pay for their own expenses'.

The Portuguese brought with them their Christian priests, and Christian missionaries soon followed to spread the Christian faith among the pagans of India. One of the earliest and most famous of these men was St. Francis Xavier. He was a Jesuit, one of the first members of this new order founded by St. Ignatius Loyola in 1540. The Jesuits were to be the most successful missionaries in the East for the next hundred years. Their letters to Europe provide much of the information we have on early contacts between East and West. When St. Francis first came ashore in Goa dressed in rags and barefoot he impressed all who saw him. He made his way straight to the hospital, then a very rough place, and washed the sores of the lepers as the first task of his mission. He preached to the poorest people, including the slaves. But what he did impressed richer people as well: they gave money to build the many fine churches in the city and also to build and equip a new hospital, one of the most modern in the world at that time. One patient there in 1608 thought it was a paradise, for each bed had cotton sheets and a silk coverlet, and on each bedside table was fresh drinking-water, a towel, a handkerchief and a fan.

The number of people actually converted to Christianity in the East was always very small. But the medical help which missionaries brought was always highly valued. St. Francis converted many people in Goa and elsewhere along the coast of India although not all of them understood what it was all about. Xavier preached without an interpreter which meant that he could not explain their new beliefs to people. He reported in one letter to Rome:

> They asked me how the soul of a dying man left his body. Was it as when we seem to be talking with friends and acquaintances in our dreams? Was this because our soul departs from our body in sleep? And, to crown all, was God black or white? For as there is so great a variety of colour among men and the Indians are themselves black, they value their own colour most highly and so believe that their gods are also black.

St. Francis taught the children songs and soon had a band of faithful followers. 'Whenever I hear of any idol-worship,' he wrote, 'I go to the place with a large band of these children who run at the idols, dash them down, break them in pieces, spit on them, trample on them, kick them about, and, in short, heap on them every possible outrage.' No doubt this was popular with the children, but it is hard to believe that it always made their parents approve of Christianity.

By 1549 Xavier was ready to move on to new lands. He left behind some native priests to carry on his work with the help of other Jesuits from Europe who had followed him to India. The most successful of all his missions was to Japan, 'The country which outdoes all others in its desire for knowledge', as he said. In 1552 he set out from Goa on his last journey, an attempt to reach China. It was not easy, for, as we shall see, China did not welcome foreign visitors. St. Francis never completed the journey. Ten years after he had arrived in Goa, he died on Shang-ch'uan, a small island off the shore of China. His body was taken to Goa for burial. There people found that it had been miraculously preserved and they put it on show once a year for several centuries. It was said to have caused many miracles so St. Francis' presence continued to affect the people of Goa. But more important was the effect of his work and that of his followers in bringing Christianity to Asia. In this way there appeared in India and the Far East for the first time a power, the Church, with the Pope at its head, which was the same for people of every language or race.

The Portuguese were busy setting up their eastern empire. As we saw, Albuquerque died convinced that the task of conquering India was almost over. But he was wrong, for while the Portuguese were capturing Goa and other ports on the west coast, another foreign race was conquering India from the north and setting up its own powerful empire there which the Portuguese never defeated. In Chapter 1 you read about Tamburlane the Great, whose conquests in Central Asia were one reason why the land-route to India and China was closed. Now his descendants were invading from the north. They were known as the Moghul emperors and they set up their empire in North India, or 'Hindustan'. A Jesuit writer told the history of their conquests very briefly as follows:

It was the King Babur Shah who invaded Hindustan... But on his death they returned and made fierce war on his son Humayun Shah... He was succeeded on the throne by Akbar who completed the conquest of the whole of Bengal. He continued his wars of conquest as long as he lived and his kingdom stretched to the sea and the territory of the King of Calicut and even as far as the island of Goa and he was greatly feared in all these lands. His court was attended by many kings, some of whom he had beaten in war while others willingly agreed to be Akbar's subjects. Sometimes as many as twenty kings were to be seen at his court, the least of whom was as powerful as the King of Calicut. In 1582 his lands stretched westwards to the Indus and north to the borders of Persia. The eastern boundary was the Bay of Bengal and on the south the sea.

The first of the Moghul Emperors, Babur Shah, was a brilliant fighter and general but also as fond of gardens as his ancestor Tamburlane had been. He kept a diary, called the

A Moghul painting of the Emperor Akbar watching elephants fighting on a floating bridge. Can you see the trees in his palace garden?

41

'Babur Nama' which he completed for almost every day of his life except when he was ill or on a particularly hard campaign. In it he recorded his first view of India:

> Hindustan is a country of few charms. Its people have no good looks; there is no civilised practice of paying calls and receiving them; there is no talent and brilliance; there are no good horses, no good dogs, no grapes, no musk-melons or first-rate fruits, no ice or cold water, no good bread or cooked food in the bazaars, no hot baths, no colleges, no candles, torches or candlesticks.

It seems surprising that Babur still thought Hindustan worth conquering. But when his conquests were over at last, he was able to turn his attention to making the country bearable to live in. He set up his capital in Agra in 1512, the year after Albuquerque conquered Malacca for the Portuguese. Here he built himself a garden and described it like this:

> The beginning, [he wrote], was made with the large well from which water flows for the hot bath and also with the piece of ground where the tamarind trees and the octagonal tank are now. After that came the large tank, or pool, with its enclosures; after that the pool in front of the outer residence; after that the house with its garden and various dwellings; after that, the hot bath. Then in that charmless and disorderly place plots of garden were seen laid out with order and symmetry with borders and lawns in every corner and in every border rose and narcissus in perfect arrangement.

The Moghul emperors all shared this love of beautiful things, books, and paintings as well as gardens. They left many fine palaces and cities, including the Taj Mahal, perhaps one of the most famous buildings in the world. And the western merchants who followed the Portuguese to India marvelled at Babur's palace at Agra and the new capital which his grandson Akbar built at Fatephur Sikri.

5 *Travellers in India*

Now that the Portuguese had an empire in India, other European merchants began to visit Goa. A Dutch traveller, Jan van Linschoten, first arrived there in 1584. He stayed for thirteen years and wrote two books about his travels which were very popular. Linschoten persuaded Dutch merchants to look for new markets in India while Richard Hakluyt encouraged traders in England by publishing his volumes of 'Travels'.

Linschoten liked his first view of Goa:

> The town is well-built with fair houses and streets in the Portuguese style. But because of the heat they are somewhat lower. They usually have their gardens and orchards at the back of their house, full of all kinds of Indian fruits; the town has all kinds of churches, like Lisbon. The island is, both summer and winter, green and always has some kind of fruit in season, which is a great pleasure; and the town lies on small hills and dales like Lisbon; it now stretches at least twice as far outside the walls as within.

The population of the island had grown quickly. Linschoten was impressed that the many different races of people there were all allowed to worship according to their own religion. But the Portuguese did insist that certain 'pagan' ceremonies should not take place in public any more, so that Christians would not be offended. Most people in Goa were merchants. Some traded by sea, buying and selling cargoes from Bengal, Burma, Malacca, even China and Japan. Or they shipped spices and other eastern goods to Europe. Others were local

The market, Goa, with slaves for sale, fine gentlemen and umbrellas. The drawing was made for Linschoten's book of travels

traders, importing goods from the mainland to feed the people of Goa. The island could not grow all it needed, so cattle, hens, hogs, eggs, milk, corn, rice and corn-oil were brought over from the mainland while olive oil was brought specially from Portugal.

Every day, starting at seven o'clock in the morning, there was a huge market in the main street. It was always over before noon when the day grew too hot. 'Those who wish to sell,' said Linschoten, 'go hanged about with all sorts of gold chains, all kinds of costly pearls, jewels, rings and precious stones, and they have running about them many sorts of slaves, both men and women, old and young which are daily sold there, as beasts are sold in Europe, where everyone may choose what he likes best. There are also Arabian horses, all kinds of spices and dried drugs, sweet gums and many curious things.' The

44   slaves who were bought and sold were an important part of

life in Goa. Some were household servants, and others were used to make goods to earn money for their masters. 'These slaves,' said Linschoten, 'fetch fresh water and sell it in the streets; the women slaves make all sorts of jams and preserves from Indian fruits and much fine needle-work. The Portuguese never work, but have their slaves to run their shops.'

The Portuguese had quickly grown used to behaving like the masters of an empire. 'When they go out in the streets,' said Linschoten, 'they step very softly and slowly forward, with a slave that carries a great hat or veil over their heads to keep the rain or sun off them. Also when it rains they commonly have a boy who bears a cloak of scarlet to cast over them: and if it is before noon, he carries a cushion for his master to kneel on at church; and his sword is carried after him so that it does not trouble him as he walks.'

The hot climate quickly made people bad-tempered. They were usually very polite, bowing and kissing their hands to each other when they met. But if someone felt that he had been insulted he would seek revenge at once. He would collect his friends and attack his enemy with bamboo sticks or bags filled with sand, leaving him half-dead. Or he would send his slaves to stab him instead. Everyone thought revenge was a matter of honour and these attacks were never punished.

Goa was governed by a Viceroy who was also the Supreme Commander of the Captains of the five Portuguese garrisons, Mozambique, Ceylon, Ormus, Malacca and Macao. He seemed to Linschoten, 'very magnificent, and goes out little. But sometimes on Sundays or Holy Days when he goes to church, the trumpets sound in the galleries of his house and he is accompanied by all the gentlemen of Goa.' Viceroys did not always govern well. In the first year a Viceroy had to 'furnish and repair his house and find out the customs of the country; in the second to gather treasure and see to his own profit [the reason he came to India] and in the third, to set all in order so as not to be taken by surprise by the new Viceroy but to return to Portugal with all the goods he could scrape together.'

Portuguese gentlemen with their servants at Goa. This drawing was also made for Linschoten's book of travels

From the time of Linschoten's visit Goa grew gradually poorer. This was partly because Linschoten himself was so successful in persuading his Dutch merchants to start trading themselves in the Indian Ocean. An English traveller, Peter Mundy, who kept a journal of his travels all his life, visited Goa in 1636 just over fifty years later. He wrote:

By report, we find that formerly the Portuguese had a flourishing time in these parts, being absolute masters and commanders of the seas, drawing all trade to them, to their incredible benefit. They spent their wealth in building churches, fair dwelling houses, rich furniture, in planting gardens, spending their time in pleasure and ease, no one to disturb them. But these days are passed, and their prosperous state much lessened by the coming of the Dutch and English who began to trade here about 40 years ago.

When he was in Goa, Linschoten met four Englishmen who had been brought for trial before the Viceroy. One of them, Ralph Fitch, wrote letters to friends in England about his adventures. On his return from the East, Richard Hakluyt also persuaded him to write about his journeys for Hakluyt's collection of famous travels. In spite of seeing Goa first from the inside of the jail, Fitch liked the town as much as Linschoten. 'It is a brave and pleasant country,' he wrote, 'and very fruitful. The summer is almost the year long, but hottest at Christmas. The day and night are all one length, and marvellous great store of fruit. For all our troubles, we are still fat and contented, for food is plentiful and very cheap.' Linschoten visited the prisoners and helped them to be released on bail. For a time they set up in business in Goa, and one of them joined the Jesuit priests to decorate the new churches with his paintings. But the others realised that the Viceroy would never allow them to leave Goa with the money that they had made. So on 5 April 1585 they set out for a picnic with plenty of provisions, leaving their shop open, to prevent anyone suspecting what they were doing. They crossed the river between Goa and the mainland (usually full of crocodiles) on foot, because it had almost run dry, and Linschoten never heard of them again.

But we know very well what happened when they had crossed the river, for Ralph Fitch reached London safely with his story in 1591. One of his companions, William Leeds, a skilled jeweller, was persuaded to stay in India to work for the Moghul Emperor, Akbar, at his new capital city of Fatephur Sikri. The leader, John Newbery, vanished on his way back to England through Persia in 1585. Fitch himself, as we shall see, had travelled through India to Burma (then called Pegu) and Malacca before his return. His first impressions of India were on his way to prison in Goa:

Here is great trade for all sorts of spices and drugs, silk and sandalwood, elephants' teeth [ivory] and much Chinese work and much sugar of the coconut. The coconut

palm is the most profitable tree in all the world. It always bears fruit and yields wine, oil, sugar, vinegar, rope, coals; of the leaves are made thatch for houses, sails for ships, mats to lie on; of the branches they make houses and brooms to sweep, of the trunk, wood for ships. Here are many Moors, and pagans. They have very strange customs among them, for they worship a cow. They will kill nothing, not so much as a louse. For they regard it as a sin to kill anything. They eat no flesh, but live on roots and rice and milk. In the towns they have hospitals to keep lame dogs and cats and birds. They give food to the ants.

Fitch's travels took him to the territory of the Moghul Emperor, Akbar, the grandson of the first emperor, Babur who built his garden at Agra:

It is a marvellous great and populous country. In their winter, which is in June, July and August, it is impossible to travel through the streets except on horseback, as the rivers run high and flood. The houses are made of clay and thatched. Here is great store of cotton cloth and rice and corn. We found many marriages both in towns and villages, of boys of eight or ten years and girls of five or six years old. They both ride upon one horse, very trimly decorated and are carried through the town with great piping and playing, and so go home and eat a banquet made of rice and fruits and there they dance the most part of the night.

He was now close to Akbar's capital, newly built for him at Fatephur Sikri and to Babur's city of Agra;

Agra is a very great and busy city built with stone, with fair, large streets, with a fair river running past it which flows into the Gulf of Bengal. It has a fair castle with a very fair ditch. The King is called Akbar; his people for

Opposite: *A Moghul painting showing the Emperor Akbar hunting with cheetahs as 'hunting dogs', as they do in Arabia. The cheetahs are hooded like hawks until they are used*

49

the most part call him the Great Moghul. From Agra we went to Fatephur which is the place where the king keeps his court. The town is bigger than Agra, but the houses and streets are not as fine. The King has in Agra and Fatephur, 1,000 elephants, 30,000 horses, 1,400 tame deer, 800 serving-women and so many leopards, tigers, buffaloes, cocks and hawks that it is very strange to see. Agra and Fatephur are much bigger than London. They have many fine carts, carved and gilded, with two wheels, drawn by two little bulls about the size of our great dogs in England. Here is a meeting place of merchants from Persia and India with silks, cloth, precious stones, rubies, diamonds and pearls. The king is clothed in a white tunic made like a shirt tied with strings at one side and a little cloth on his head often coloured red or yellow. I left William Leeds, the jeweller, in service with the King Akbar at Fatephur, who did treat him very well and gave him a house and five slaves, a horse and every day six silver pieces.

Fitch later visited Bengal, stopping at the Holy City of Benares on the River Ganges:

In this river Ganges there are many islands. His water is very sweet and the country beside it very fruitful. Benares is a great town and a great deal of cotton cloth is made there and Turbans for the Moors. To this town the pagans [Hindus] come on pilgrimage from far away. Along the water there are many fair houses and in all of them images of the gods standing, made of stone and wood, some like lions, leopards and monkeys, some like women and men and peacocks and some like the devil with four arms and four hands. By break of day and before, there are men and women who come out of the town and wash themselves in the Ganges.

Although he was very interested in all the marvels of India, 50 Fitch was firstly a merchant. He had come to find spices which

Gathering pepper for a European trader

made such a valuable part of the cargoes sailors brought home to Europe. He described what he had discovered about the chief spices, like this:

> The pepper grows in many parts of India, especially around Cochin. And much of it grows wild in the fields among the bushes without any labour. When it is ripe they go and gather it. The shrub is like our ivy tree and if it did not grow up some tree or pole it would fall down and rot. When they first gather it, it is green; and then they lay it in the sun and it becomes black. The ginger grows like our garlic and the root is the ginger; it is to be found in many parts of India. The cloves come from the islands of the Moluccas which are several islands; their tree is like our bay tree. The nutmegs and mace grow together and come from the island of Banda; the tree is like our walnut tree but somewhat smaller.

Fitch had learnt that some of the spices sold in Indian markets had already been brought hundreds of miles from the Spice Islands, the East Indies. Like other merchants he set out east to look for them.

6   *Merchants Reach the Spice Islands*

The first sailors to the East after Vasco da Gama's great voyage were still not sure where the Spice Islands lay. As they found their way to the ports of Burma, Siam and Malacca they soon learned the names of other countries further east. But it was not easy to tell where they were for there were no charts to help them. It took some time to discover where the mainland ended and islands began, as you will see if you look at the map on page 70. An early writer about Portugal's discoveries in the East, in a book published in 1563, thought of a way to help his readers to imagine the shapes of these new countries. You may like to try it:

> Place your left hand turned palm downwards with the fingers pointing towards your body, and you have in front of you a rough map of the coastline from India to Vietnam and China. The thumb, spaced apart from the index finger, represents India, and the space in between stands for the Bay of Bengal. The index finger, which should be spread apart from the remaining fingers, represents the Malay peninsula. The three remaining fingers should be pressed together and slightly drawn up underneath the palm to represent the Indochina peninsula [modern Cambodia and Vietnam] and show its more northerly position and its northerly slant.

Even when they had found their way round the coasts of Sumatra and through the Straits of Malacca as far as the

Opposite: *An early sixteenth century map of India and the Spice Islands. Can you find Ceylon, Sumatra, Borneo and the Moluccas? They are not spelt as they are today*

islands of the Moluccas and the Philippines, sailors could never be sure of finding a port in which to anchor. Some countries, Java or Pegu (the old name for Burma), were very civilised and powerful nations, while Malacca was one of the greatest trading cities in the world at that time. But others were still inhabited by savage tribes. Ralph Fitch set out for Pegu on 28 November 1586:

> From Bengal to Pegu is 90 leagues. We came to Cosmin which is a very pretty town and stands very pleasantly, very well supplied with everything. The people are very tall and friendly, the women white, round-faced, with little eyes: the houses are built high up, set on great posts and they reach them with long ladders for fear of the tigers which are very many. The country is very fruitful in all things, figs, oranges, coconuts and other fruits. The land is very low-lying and full of rivers and they all go to and fro in boats which they call 'paroes' and use as their houses with their wives and children in them.

Fitch also visited Dela 'which is a very fair town and has a fair port where many ships set out for Malacca, Mecca and other places. Here are eighteen or twenty very great and long houses where they tame and keep many elephants for the King. For it is in the wild country around that they catch them.'

Fitch soon reached Pegu which was the capital city of the country of the same name:

> Pegu is very great and strong and fair, with walls of stone and great ditches round about it. There are two towns, the old town and the new. In the old town are all the foreign merchants as well as those of Pegu. All the goods are sold in the old town which is very great and has many suburbs round about it and all the houses are made of canes which they call bamboos and are covered with straw. In your house you have a warehouse which they call a 'Godown' which is built of brick to keep your goods in. For they often catch fire and in an hour four or five

54

Gathering coconuts, bananas, areca nuts and pepper (which grows like ivy up the palm tree). This picture also comes from Linschoten's book of travels

hundred houses may burn; so that without the 'godown' you would be in danger of losing everything if the wind rose. In the new town is the King and all his nobles and gentry. It is a very big city with many people, built in a square with very fair walls and a great ditch round it full of water with many crocodiles in it. There are also towers for sentinels made of wood and gilded with gold. The streets are as fair as any I have ever seen, as straight as a line from one gate to the other and so broad that ten men may ride abreast in them. On both sides at every man's door is set a palm tree which makes a very broad and convenient shadow so that a man may walk in the shade all day. The king's house is in the middle, walled and ditched and richly gilded. Within the first gate is a great, large room on both sides of which are houses for the King's elephants, which are trained for wars and in the King's service. Among the rest he has four white elephants which

55

are very rare, for no other king has them. If any other king does have one, he sends to him to ask for it. When any of these white elephants is brought, all the merchants are commanded to come and see them and to give the King a present of half-a-ducat, which comes to a great sum, for there are many merchants in the city. After this they may come and see them when they like. This King's title is 'King of the White Elephants'. If another king will not send him a white elephant he will make war on him for he would rather lose a great part of his kingdom than not conquer him. They treat these elephants with great reverence; each one stands in a house gilded with gold and they feed out of dishes of silver and gilt. When one of them goes to the river to be washed, as they do every day, he has a cover of cloth-of-gold or silk held over him by 6 or 8 men and 8 or 10 men go ahead, playing on drums and trumpets. And there is a gentleman who washes his feet in a silver basin.

Close to the great and civilised countries like Pegu, up and down the coasts of Sumatra and further east, lay islands inhabited by primitive tribes. Cesar Frederik, a Venetian traveller described the Andaman islanders off the west coast of Sumatra:

They call these people savages because they eat one another. also these islands go to war with each other, for they have small boats and with them they capture each other and so eat each other. And if by evil chance any ship is wrecked on these islands, as many have been, there is not one man of these ships lost there that escapes uneaten or unslain.

The Portuguese originally came to the Indian Ocean looking for Christians and spices. By 1511 they had conquered Malacca at the eastern edge of the Ocean and set up their own garrison there. In 1518 they began to explore further east. They first went to the Moluccas, a group of islands to the south of the Philippines, where cloves were grown. The news of their victory at Malacca in 1511 had already reached these far-off islands and their rulers hoped to make peace with the Portuguese. The first Portuguese expedition was led by Antonius Abreu. He sailed from Java to Amboina, setting up stone pillars along the coast and charting his way just as Bartholemew Diaz had done along the coast of Africa. The next port of call was a group of islands known as Banda, the only place in the world at that time where nutmeg and a spice called mace were grown. Mace was particularly good for disguising the taste of meat that had begun to go bad.

When Abreu reached the Moluccas, a war had broken out between the rulers of the two larger islands of Tidore and Ternate as to which should be the ally of the Portuguese traders. While they were busy fighting each other Abreu took control of all the Moluccas in the name of the King of Portugal.

Now that the Portuguese had ports and garrisons in the places where spices were grown, they could also control any foreign merchants who wished to trade there. The garrison at Malacca was never very large, but the trade which passed through the port between India and China and Japan soon became a very large part of the business which made merchants in Goa and Lisbon so rich. Portugal continued to be the chief supplier of spices, drugs, cottons and precious stones to Europe until the end of the fifteenth century. But the chief profits from the trade in the Indian Ocean were not from selling European goods there (for no one wanted them), but from trading one eastern product with another.

As we have seen in India, the Portuguese were not left alone for long to enjoy the riches of their trade. English and Dutch merchants soon came to take a share for themselves. At first they simply took it by piracy as we can see in this account of an English voyage to the East Indies in 1592:

The 2nd of February 1592, we set sail straight to the East Indies; but having calms and contrary winds, it was not until the month of June that we reached the coast of India near Calicut; because of this many of our men died from lack of fresh supplies. In the month of June we anchored at

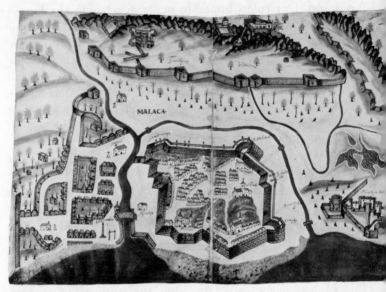

Malacca in the sixteenth century

the islands of Pulao Pinaom where we stayed until the first day of September, our men being very sick and dying rapidly. This day we set sail to Malacca. And we had not been long at sea when we took a ship of the kingdom of Pegu of some eighty tons with wooden-anchors and about 50 men in her with a pinnace about 18 tons at her stern both laden with pepper. Here we might have taken two more ships of Pegu laden with pepper and rice. In this month also we took a great Portuguese ship of six or seven hundred tons, loaded chiefly with food, chests of hats, and cloth. Besides this we took another Portuguese ship of some hundred tons loaded with food, rice, cloth and other goods. These ships were bound for Malacca with supplies, for the people of Goa and other places in India supply Malacca with food, because food there is very scarce.

In the month of November 1592 we set our course for the Nicobar islands some miles to the north-west of the famous island of Sumatra, where we anchored. Here we obtained very good supplies, for the people (whom we found to be Moslems) came alongside with their canoes with hens, plantains [bananas], and other fruits; and within two days they brought us royals [a kind of coin] of gold plate, which they found by diving in the sea; for the coins were lost not long before from two Portuguese ships wrecked there on their way to China. This was the furthest place that we reached to the south-east.

Stories like this one were collected by Richard Hakluyt in England (you can read about him in the How Do We Know? section) and by Linschoten in Holland. The stories were meant to encourage English and Dutch merchants to join in the eastern trade for themselves. They described rich cargoes and set out practical advice for reaching the markets where they could be bought. They passed on to their readers some of the knowledge that Portuguese explorers had gained. The Portuguese had tried to keep this knowledge to themselves so that they alone might profit from the eastern trade. Their maps, log-books and journals were presented to the royal libraries in Lisbon. There they had collected secret information on harbours, anchorages, shoals and trade winds; the skill of their pilots became so famous in the East as well as the West that the Emperor of Japan made a law that all his ships were to carry Portuguese pilots. Hakluyt provided his readers with notes on the trade winds and the eastern windy and rainy seasons known as *monsoons*. By keeping notes of the dates on which these winds appeared every year he even worked out timetables for voyages to and from the Indian Ocean.

As Hakluyt was particularly interested in obtaining the secret information of the Portuguese, he was very pleased when Sir Francis Drake captured a huge Portuguese carrack on its way back from the Far East in 1587. Carracks were far larger than the 'naus' built for Vasco da Gama's voyage. They were built of a hard eastern wood called teak brought from Pegu, in the Portuguese ship-yards at Goa. They were between 1,200 and 1,600 tons, perhaps the largest ships ever seen at that time.

A carrack built to carry large cargoes. It was heavily armed against pirates

When they sailed home from Goa to Lisbon with their priceless cargoes, Dutch and English pirate ships usually left them alone. Drake was the first to attack one successfully. The booty which Drake's sailors won was huge. It would have been worth nearly a million pounds today. But some of the most valuable prizes were the maps, charts and log-books that the ship carried. Hakluyt thought it most important:

> It is to be noted that the taking of this carrack had two extraordinary effects in England, first that it taught others that carracks were no such bugs but that they might be taken, [he means that they were not too big and frightening to be captured] and secondly in showing the English people the details of the enormous riches and wealth of the East Indies. This has encouraged the English and their neighbours in Holland, being men as skilful in navigation and quite as courageous as the Portuguese, to share with them in the East Indies; where they discover that the Portuguese are not at all as strong as they had thought.

So Portugal did not have the East Indies to themselves for long. While they did, the centre of their power there was the port of Malacca. Let us see what Ralph Fitch has to say of it in the account of his travels which Richard Hakluyt persuaded him to write:

> And so to Malacca the eighth of February 1587, where the Portuguese have a castle which stands by the sea. And the country round the town belongs to the Malays which are a proud people. They go naked with a cloth about their middle and a little roll of cloth about their heads. Many ships come here from China and the Moluccas, Banda, Timor and the other islands with great store of spices, drugs, diamonds and other jewels. The voyages into many of these islands are under the control of the Captain of the Malacca garrison; so that no one can go there without his permission. For these traders pay great sums of money every year.

Linschoten, the Dutchman who helped Fitch when he was in prison in Goa, also visited Malacca and wrote about all the countries of South-east Asia. He tells us that Malacca had only quite recently been inhabited when the Portuguese arrived. It was once just a group of fishermens' huts, but Malay traders had set up a port there. The coming of the Portuguese had made Moslem traders move further eastwards from their old markets on the coast of India. The Portuguese found that wherever they travelled into south-east Asia, their hated rivals, the Moslems, had gone there before them. Many of the original inhabitants had been converted to the Moslem faith and did not want to listen to the Christian missionaries who came with the Portuguese.

Not many Portuguese chose to live in Malacca for, as Linschoten explained, 'it is a very unhealthy country, for natives as well as foreigners so that it is only because of profit that people will stay there.' Malacca had no crops or products itself, but 'everything is brought there in great abundance and there is every year a ship from Portugal which sets out a month 61

Pearl divers off the coast of Ceylon

before those sailing to India, which is loaded at Malacca with twice as costly merchandise and spices as any loaded in India.' In the harbour there were ships of every nation:

> four-masted *junks* with cargoes of sugar, great stores of raw silk, porcelain, damasks, *musks*, rhubarb, silver, pearls, gilded chests, fans and other objects. In exchange for these the Chinese take away pepper, incense, saffron, coral, mercury, opium, drugs. From Malacca ships sail to the Moluccas for cloves, to Timor for sandalwood, to Banda for nutmegs and mace; and all through the islands of the Javas is sold Indian cloth, porcelain from China, iron knives, drugs and gold from Sumatra.

There was so much gold in Malacca that the chief merchants kept their accounts in bars of gold and could unload a ship and reload it with precious goods entirely from their own warehouses.

7 Furthest East, Where Portugal and Spain Meet

The gold of Malacca made the risk of illness and death in its terrible climate worthwhile. Merchants filled its harbour from East and West. But for many poor sailors all that the great new markets of the East could offer was disaster from shipwreck or a slow and lingering death from scurvy. On Linschoten's first voyage to Goa, 'There died on our ship thirty persons, among which some were slaves, and one high Dutchman that had been in the King of Spain's guard. Every man had been sick once or twice and let blood. This is commonly the number that ordinarily died in the ships. In one extraordinary plague there died 900, all thrown into the sea before they came to Mozambique, the Viceroy being one.'

The merchants at home in Europe who provided the ships and their goods took their share of risks. They might be bankrupted in a year by storms or pirates. But if even one ship returned safely with a cargo of eastern luxuries it would more than repay a year's expenses. While the sailors and merchants struggled to survive and grow rich, the wealth and power of their different countries grew as well. Kings still urged their subjects on to discover new lands and new markets. That is how the Portuguese and the Spaniards who had already divided the Atlantic Ocean between them met again on the shores of the Pacific.

For the Portuguese, the route East beyond Malacca lay through a new landscape quite strange to European travellers. This was the area of swamps and islands which made up the Malay *Archipelago*. Peter Mundy was one English sailor who travelled this way. He reached China and returned to England 63 in 1636 with a journal of his travels and sketches that he had made on the way. Here he describes the route through the Straits of Singapore, off the coast of Malaya. 'This mainland is like the island of Sumatra, clouds and fogs usually hanging over the lowland as well as the tops of the hills. This makes the country rich in trees, grass and green things as well as in fountains and springs, although the climate is thought to be unhealthy.' He sailed south and found himself surrounded by:

> many boats with excellent good fresh fish and dried. We went 4 or 5 leagues with all the way on both sides so full of creeks, passages and islands, that I never saw the like, like so many haystacks laid close together all overgrown with trees. Here we saw several groups of small boats covered with mats which is the ordinary housing of those who live here. They brought us fish, killing them with fishing spears, and a pretty sport it is to see them pursue the fish with their little boats for the fish scud before them as porpoises do before the stem of a ship in a gale; they also brought us bananas, sugar-cane and pineapples.

The travellers soon came to the island of Java. But Javanese merchants preferred to carry on their trade at Malacca and European ships only stopped there for urgent supplies. Perhaps it was because, as Linschoten said, 'the Javanese are of a very fretful and obstinate nature.' They now sailed for over 150 kilometres, 'between many islands and through many shallows where they had to anchor every night to avoid the danger of sandbanks'. Then, as Linschoten wrote:

> east by north-east to Banda, where are the best nutmegs and flowers and they make oil of them which is brought to Malacca. The trade here consists chiefly in bartering, but the people are not to be trusted. You must keep careful watch and not go ashore, for my friend, a captain in a ship, being there, he was captured with all his men and put in prison for 2 years. There he endured a terrible life but in the end was ransomed. All of these voyages can only be

undertaken with special licence from the King of Portugal, given as a reward for some service performed in the Indies.

The last port of call in the East was the islands of the Moluccas. Their only product was the clove, but as it did not grow anywhere else, Portuguese merchants shared the simple life of these primitive islanders for a time in order to obtain it. Linschoten described the country as 'fiery hills, a very dry and burnt land, no food but flesh or fish: some rice, corn, garlic, onions and suchlike are brought from Portugal. They barter them for cloves. The bread which they make there is of wood or roots [tapioca] and their clothes of woven straw or herbs, fair to the eye.'

These small islands with their single crop were the cause of

Linschoten's picture of Malays, the most civilised peoples of the East Indies, and the proud, 'stiff-necked' Javanese

fierce fighting between Portugal and her old rival, Spain. The explorer Magellan was the first to claim the Moluccas for Spain. It was only after several fights and the sinking of each other's ships that peace was made. In 1529 a treaty was signed at Saragossa in Spain, giving the Moluccas to Portugal in exchange for a large payment to Spain. The Spanish were free to explore islands to the north-east, such as the Philippines which had first been discovered by Magellan in 1521.

These islands were finally conquered and settled by Spanish ships sailing from New Spain (or Mexico) in the 1560s. They were governed from the capital, Manila, by a Spanish Governor. Linschoten described the Philippines as very pleasant:

> It is a very fruitful land and has much corn and all sorts of beasts such as deer, cattle, buffaloes, oxen, hogs, goats. They have many musk-cats (used to make perfume) all kinds of fruit as in China, honey and fish. The Chinese trade there and bring all sorts of goods, such as silks, cottons, porcelain, gunpowder, *sulphur*, *brimstone*, iron, steel, mercury, copper, *chestnuts* and suchlike. There come every year from China at least 20 ships. Then goods are shipped from the Philippines to Mexico. This route is now as common as the route from India to Portugal.

The Spanish made sure of their share in the spice trade with the East. It was highly organised and its merchants grew very rich. Here is a letter from a Spaniard to his father in 1590, two years after the defeat of the Great Armada. It is clear that English pirates were one of the many dangers to sailors in the Pacific as well as in the Indian Ocean.

> All the merchants of Mexico bring their Spanish goods down to Acapulco harbour to ship them to China. From here to China is about 2,000 leagues farther than from Mexico to Spain. It takes 13 or 14 months to sail from here to China and return. I can tell you one thing; that 200 ducats in Spanish goods and some Flemish wares which I took with me to Mexico, I traded for 1,400 ducats worth

66

of goods in China. So I reckon that with these silks and other goods that I brought with me from China to Mexico I earned 2,500 ducats by the voyage; and would have had more if one pack of fine silks had not been spoiled with salt water. So, as I said, there is great gain to be got if a man return in safety. But in 1588 [the year of the Great Armada] I was very unlucky coming in a ship from China to Mexico: it was loaded with rich goods when it was taken by an English ship which robbed us and after burned our boat in which I lost a great deal of treasure.

As for the Philippines, it is the goodliest country and the richest in all the world. For here are great store of gold mines, silver mines, pearls, great store of cotton cloth: for the country people wear nothing else but fine cotton which is more popular than silk. Here there is a great supply of silk, all very cheap. All kinds of food, such as bread, flesh, fish, wine and hens and all kinds of fowl are very plentiful. Here are great store of fresh rivers. The people are very loving. Here are fair cities and towns with costly buildings better than those in Spain. And the country people are very richly clothed both in silks and gold. But here we have orders from the King of Spain that a Spaniard may not live in the Philippines for more than three years and afterwards they must return to Mexico and other soldiers must come in their place. The country is very unhealthy for us Spaniards. For within these twenty years, of 14,000 men who have gone to the Philippines, there are 13,000 of them dead and not more than 1,000 of them left alive.

For all nations the risks of trading in the East Indies were very, very high. But the fortunes that could be gained made them worth taking.

8 China, the Country that Must Be Seen

In 1508 the Portuguese were already curious to find out about China. King Manuel sent a squadron of four ships from Lisbon with orders to visit Madagascar, Ceylon and Malacca. They had orders to 'ask after the Chins [or Chinese] where they come from, when they come to Malacca, the goods they bring, the build of their ships, if they have houses in Malacca, if they are weak men or warriors, what clothes they wear and if they are big men...also if they are Christians or heathens and if their country is a very big one, if they have more than one king, what they do worship and what customs they observe.' That is a very long list of questions. Unfortunately we do not know if King Manuel's sailors were able to answer them.

Chinese junks were often in the port of Malacca. So in 1508 the Portuguese did find their 'Chins' there and had several friendly meetings with them. After the conquest of the city, when a Portuguese camp had been established there in 1511, they began to find out more about the mysterious empire in the East. The first Portuguese ship reached the coast of China in 1514 and reported:

> The merchants of China also make voyages to Malacca across the Great Gulf to obtain cargoes of spices and to bring from their own country musk, rhubarb, pearls, tin, porcelain and silk. For they are a people of great skill like ourselves, but uglier to look at, with little bits of eyes. During this last year some of our Portuguese made a visit to China. They were not allowed to land for they say it is against their custom to allow foreigners to enter their cities. But they sold their goods at a great profit; there is as great

a profit in taking spices to China as in taking them to Portugal, for it is a cold country and they make great use of them.

Encouraged by this start the Portuguese sent an official embassy to China. Their fleet landed at Canton and the ambassador Tomas Pires was allowed to travel to Peking to meet the emperor himself. Here he waited, while the fleet traded profitably with the merchants of Canton and returned to Malacca. But now things began to go wrong. The Chinese emperor, Cheng-te, died. Naturally no ambassadors could be received while the Court was in mourning, so the Chinese sent Pires back to Canton. Meanwhile a second Portuguese fleet had arrived, but its leader was behaving very badly. The Chinese in Canton reported his arrival as follows:

Unloading large cargo-junks in a Chinese port

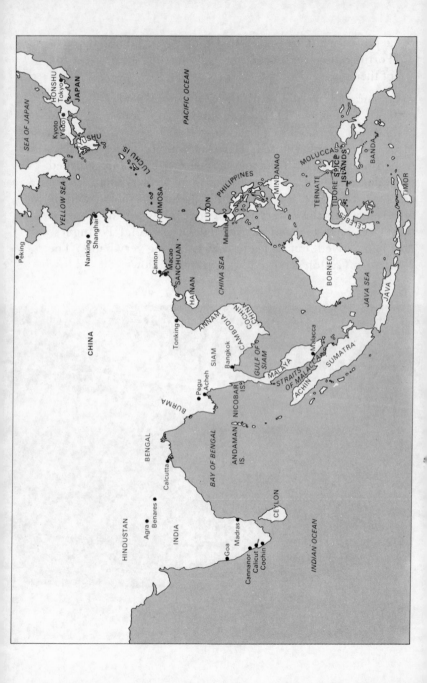

Some time near the end of Cheng-te's reign a people not recognised as *tributary* to China, known as the Feringhis [Portuguese], together with a crowd of riff-raff made their way into the harbours near Canton and set up a barracks and a fort, mounted many cannon to make war, captured islands, killed people, robbed ships and terrified the population along the coasts. As they wanted to take some land for themselves they set up boundary stones and tried to control other foreign traders in the area.

The Chinese naturally turned against all 'Feringhis' and Pires and his companions were tortured and imprisoned in Canton. They smuggled out letters which were published in Europe, giving details of their imprisonment and of their experiences in Peking. The Portuguese who came back to trade in 1521 were attacked by the Chinese as 'fan-kuei' or 'foreign devils' and driven out. It seemed as if trade with China was at an end. So it was, officially—but the Chinese coastline had many secret harbours and offshore islands and Portuguese merchants soon joined in the smuggling that was a profitable business there. The chief imports to China were pepper and ivory. In the winter of 1548, when the Portuguese had finished trading for the year they set sail for Malacca. They left behind two junks loaded with the goods they had not yet sold. On board were thirty Portuguese including a man called Galeote Pereira. Unfortunately the Chinese had just formed a special coastguard fleet to deal with pirates. In March 1549 this fleet captured the junks. The Portuguese, including Pereira, were carried off in cages to the city of Foochow where they stayed in prison for over a year. Most of them were executed but a few survivors were exiled to the city of Kweilin in the south-west of China. Here news of them reached the Portuguese traders off the south China coast who made arrangements to help them to escape and Pereira reached the offshore island of Shang-ch'uan at about the time that St. Francis Xavier died there.

He wrote an account of his imprisonment which was published in 1561. It was quickly translated into English and Hakluyt included it in his volume of travels. (You will find other descriptions of China in the sixteenth century in 'Barbarians in Peking', another book in the Then and There Series.) Pereira was particularly interested in the way China was governed by the Emperor with the help of officials chosen by

A Chinese magistrate at his desk, with pens, ink-block and paper

their success in an examination held regularly throughout China: 'Many things are asked them, ' he said, 'and if they answer correctly and are found good enough to take their degree they receive a cap and girdle which shows everyone that they have become a member of the scholar-class. From this class the Emperors' officials are selected—they are treated with the greatest respect.' Pereira was also impressed by Chinese good manners:

The scholars and all the people of China eat their food sitting on stools at high tables as we do, and very cleanly too, although they do not use tablecloths or napkins. Whatever is put on the table is carved before it is brought in; they feed with two sticks, without touching their food with their hands, just as we do with forks. Nor are they only polite at meals, but also in conversation and courtesy they seem better than all other nations.

Life in a Chinese prison was not pleasant, but Pereira still admired Chinese courts and justice:

We poor strangers could say what we liked...yet they treated us so patiently that they made us wonder, knowing especially how badly any judge in our country would treat us. For we, having as our enemies two of the chiefest men in a whole town and without an interpreter and ignorant of the language did in the end see our great enemies put in prison because of us, and deprived of their jobs and honour because they did not do justice, and even likely to die; for as the people say, they will be beheaded.

Pereira admired China in other ways, too:

This country is so well inhabited near the sea-coast that you cannot go a mile without seeing some town or village ...But those who dwell in the country are very poor, for the multitude of them is everywhere so great, that out of a tree you will many times see swarm a number of children where a man would not have thought to have found any at all. The streets are everywhere well-paved with squared stones except where for want of stone they use brick. There is not one foot of ground in which crops are not grown. One ox draws the plough alone...these countrymen do by art in farming that which we have to do by force. There is great abundance of hens, geese, ducks, swine and goats; sheep have they none. Two pounds [four kilograms] of hen's flesh, or goose or duck is worth two 'fen' of their money which is a penny...The cities are very fine, 73

The river-front at K'ai-feng with shops and river-boats

especially near the gates which are marvellously high and covered with iron. The gatehouses are built on high with towers...besides the many market-places in which all things are on sale, through every street there go hawkers continually crying their wares, such as flesh of all sorts, fresh fish, herbs, oil, vinegar, meal, rice, in short all things so plentifully that many houses need no servants, everything being brought to their doors. It is wonderful to see how great these cities are, and the cause is that the houses are built evenly, and take a great deal of space.

Shortly after Pereira's escape from China in 1553, the Chinese began quietly and unofficially to trade more freely with the Portuguese. In 1554 the captain of the Malacca garrison made an agreement with the captain of the Chinese

Camels leaving through the gate of K'ai-feng in a busy street of traders.

coastguard fleet that the Portuguese might be allowed to trade. At first their base was on the island of Shang-ch'uan where St. Francis Xavier had died and Pereira had gone after his escape from prison. But in 1558 they were allowed to move to Macao just off the mainland of China. By 1569 their garrison at Macao had grown to be 'a very large settlement with three churches and a hospital for the poor'. But it was still an unofficial settlement, part of an agreement with the Governor of Kwangsi province in South China. The Portuguese were allowed to stay on the mainland in exchange for their help in dealing with Japanese pirates. The Emperor of China knew nothing about this arrangement, as we can see from a letter written by the Spanish Governor of the Philippines in 1582:

The Portuguese of Macao are still without any weapons or

gunpowder, nor justice, having a Chinese *Mandarin* who searches their houses to see if they have any such. And because it is a regular town with about 500 houses and there is a Portuguese governor and a bishop there, they pay every three years to the new Viceroy of Canton about 100,000 ducats to avoid being expelled from the land. This sum he divides with the grandees of the household of the King of China. However, it is agreed by everyone that the King has no idea that there are any such Portuguese in the land.

By the early seventeenth century when Peter Mundy visited Macao, the town was well-established (see the picture below). 'Macao', he wrote in his Journal, 'stands at one end of a great island built on rising ground, some gardens and trees among their houses making a pretty sight, somewhat like Goa [see the picture on page 36] though not so big; their houses double-tiled and plastered over again for prevention

A plan of Macao in the late sixteenth century

of hurricanes or violent winds that happen some years called by the Chinese "*Typhoons*", which is also the reason (they say) they build no high towers nor steeples to their churches.' Mundy was entertained to an official banquet in Macao:

> At our landing on the shore we were received by the Council and the Elders of the city, leading us into a very fair house richly furnished. Our dinner was served in silver plate, very good and savoury to my mind, but the manner of it much differing from ours. For every man had a similar portion of food brought between two plates and this often changed, for before the man had finished with the one, there was another plate stood before him. Every man had his silver goblet by his plate, which was no sooner empty but there stood ready those that filled them up again with excellent good Portuguese wine. There was also not very good music of voice, harp and guitar.

Mundy enjoyed rather more another performance he saw in Macao:

> Our Admirals, etc. were invited ashore by the Jesuit Fathers to see a play to be acted in St. Paul's Church by the children of the town, there being a hundred that should act. It was part of the life of this much-renowned saint, Francis Xavier, in which there were several pretty passages, viz—a Chinese dance by children in Chinese costume; a battle between the Dutch and the Portuguese, where the Dutch were overcome, (but without any speeches or actions to disgrace the Dutch); another dance of large crabs, being so many boys very prettily and wittily disguised as crabs, who all sang and played on musical instruments as if they had been so many crabs.

The wealth of Macao came from goods which the Portuguese bought and sold in Asia. Very few goods were brought from Europe for sale in the East, although Chinese goods like porcelain and silk were sold in Europe, as well as the spices on which European cooks relied. Portuguese ships trading

77

between Goa and Macao were loaded with Indian spices and drugs and cotton cloth, as these were very popular with the Chinese. But the greatest fortunes of all were to be made by trading between China and Japan. As these countries were officially at war, they could not buy and sell directly with each other, but each wanted what the other could provide. The Japanese loved Chinese silks and the Chinese needed Japanese silver. The Portuguese took Chinese silk to Japan and came back with silver for China, and the merchants of Macao grew very rich. Let us see how Ralph Fitch described this trade in 1584:

The ship that goes every year from the Indies to China is called the ship of Drugs, because she carries different drugs of India, but the greatest part of her cargo is silver. From Malacca it is 18,000 miles [30,000 kilometres]: and from China to Japan every year a ship of great importance sails loaded with silk. In exchange for this they bring bars of silver which they trade with China. The distance between China and Japan is 2,400 miles [3,900 kilometres], with several islands on the way. From these islands onwards the seas are not yet explored, because of the great shoals of sand which they find. The Portuguese have made a small city near to the coast of China called Macao, whose buildings and houses are made of wood. It hath a bishop, but the customs dues are paid to the King of China and they go and pay the same at a city called Canton. This is a city of great importance and very beautiful, two and a half day's journey from Macao. The people of China are pagans and are so jealous and fearful that they do not want a stranger to put his foot in their land: so that when the Portuguese go to Canton to pay their customs and to buy their merchandize they will not allow them to stay within the city, but send them out into the suburbs. The country of China is of very great importance, which may be judged by the rich and precious merchandize which comes from thence, than which I believe there are not better nor richer in the world beside. First, great store of gold which they carry to India, made in plates like to little ships, and in value 23 *carats* apiece. Then very great abundance of fine silk, cloth of damask and taffeta, great quantity of musk, quicksilver [mercury] and cinnabar [mercuric oxide], great store of *camphor*, an infinite quantity of porcelain made in vessels of different sorts; and every year there comes to the Indies from China two or three great ships loaded with most rich and precious cargo.

Macao remained the centre of European trade with China for many years to come, although the Portuguese had to share their port with their Dutch and English rivals. Accounts of China and her wonders made a great impression in Europe and Chinese goods became very popular. A simple porcelain dish was so rare that it was thought to be a suitably rich dish for Queen Elizabeth I. She had already shown her interest in the country by sending a letter to the Emperor of China with the explorer John Newbery when he set out for India with Ralph Fitch. It was never delivered, as we know, because Newbery hardly travelled further east than Goa.

By the eighteenth century, China was so fashionable that European gardens, palaces and furnishings were often designed 'in the Chinese taste', that is, in the Chinese fashion; and European philosophers spoke with enthusiasm of the noble system of government in the Chinese empire. China impressed those who visited her, as well. A Dominican friar who spent much of his life as a missionary in the East wrote the following introduction to his account of his Chinese travels, in 1570:

Whereas distant things often sound greater than they really are, in this case it is exactly the opposite. For China is much more than it sounds and the sight of it makes a very different impression from what is heard or read about it, as is agreed to be true by myself and others, after we have seen the things of China. This must be seen and not heard, because hearing is nothing in comparison with seeing it.

9 The Best Who have yet been Discovered – Europeans Reach Japan

King Manuel gave Portuguese explorers special orders to search for the Chinese. But the Japanese were discovered by accident. Tomé Pires, the first European ambassador to China in 1518, describes some merchants called 'Guores', almost certainly Japanese. But little seemed to be known of their homeland and no one connected them with the people of 'Cipangu' an island which Marco Polo had mentioned in his 'Travels'. Then in 1542, three Portuguese merchants on a Chinese junk ran into a typhoon, a terrible tropical storm off the south coast of China. An official Portuguese historian tells the story;

> In the year 1542 three Portuguese companions were in the port of Siam with their junk, carrying on their trade. They decided to go to China because of its being a voyage of much profit. And loading their ship with hides and other goods they set sail and with fair weather crossed the great Gulf of Hainan and gave a wide berth to the city of Canton as they could not enter the city. The Portuguese became so detested that the King of China commanded 'that the men with beards and large eyes should not be permitted within his realms', and inscribed this on large letters of gold and fixed it to the gates of Canton. And their junk ran into a fearful storm of the kind the natives call a 'typhoon', which is fierce and appalling. It makes such thundering and quaking that it seems as if all the spirits of Hell are whirling the waves and the sea, whose fury seems to cause flashes of fire in the sky. And in the space of an hour-

glass the wind blows from all the points of the compass in turn and seems to blow stronger in each one of them. This tempest lasted 24 hours and at the end the junk stopped pitching and tossing; but it was left in such a state that there was nothing for it but to let the wind blow it where it liked; which at the end of fifteen days drove it between some islands where they landed not knowing where they were. From the land small boats put out at once to meet them in which came men whiter than the Chinese, but with small eyes and short beards. From them they learned that these islands were called Nipongi, which we commonly call Japan. And finding that these people were kind, they went ashore with them and were very hospitably received. Here they repaired their junk and exchanged their goods for silver; and as it was then the season, they returned to Malacca.

After this happy outcome to their troubles the Portuguese lost no time in coming back to Japan. A merchant called Pero Diez who sailed to Japan on one of these early voyages in 1544 has left us the first eyewitness account of the country and the people, in a report he wrote for the King of Portugal:

It is a very cold country; the villages on the coast are small and on each island there is a chief. The inhabitants are good-looking, white and bearded with shaven heads. They read and write in the same way as do the Chinese. They keep many horses on which they ride. Their stirrups are of copper. The working people wear woollen clothes; the superior classes are dressed in silk, brocade, satin and taffeta; the women mostly have very white complexions and are very beautiful. The houses are built of stone and clay, the interior is plastered and the roofs are covered with tiles in the same manner as in our country, and they have upper floors, windows and galleries. They keep hawks for hunting but they do not use the meat of cattle for food. They cultivate the ground with oxen and ploughs. They use leather shoes and small hats of horsehair. They

A Japanese Screen showing Jesuit priests (on the far right) and Portuguese merchants landing in Japan

bid each other farewell with great courtesy. There is plenty of fishing. The wealth they possess consists of silver which is found in small *ingots*, of which a sample was sent to Your Majesty.

The Japanese were curious about their foreign visitors as well, but not always so polite. One Japanese writer described them like this:

These men are traders of Seinamban [Southwest Barbary]. They understand to a certain degree the difference between Superior and Inferior, but I do not know whether they have a proper system of ceremonial behaviour. They eat

82

with their fingers instead of with chopsticks such as we use. They show their feelings without any self-control. They cannot understand the meaning of written characters. They are a people who spend their whole lives roving about, bartering things they have for those they do not, but for all that they are a harmless sort of people.

This low opinion of Europeans did not stop a Japanese called Yajiro from travelling to Malacca in 1547 to meet the missionary, St. Francis Xavier. He became the first Christian convert from Japan and St. Francis was so pleased with him that he decided to visit Japan himself. For the next fifty years, 83 missionaries were to play as important a part as merchants in the trade with Japan. Xavier himself reached Japan in 1549 and reported enthusiastically:

> By the experience we have had I can inform you–firstly, the people we have met with so far are the best who have as yet been discovered, and it seems to me we shall never find among heathens another race to equal the Japanese. They are men of honour to a marvel and prize honour above all else in the world. Those who are not of gentle birth pay much honour to the gentry who in their turn pride themselves on faithfully serving their feudal lord to whom they are very obedient. They are small eaters, although somewhat heavy drinkers. They swear but little and when they do it is by the sun. There are many who can read and write which is a great help to their learning prayers and religious matters. There are but few thieves, because thieves' lives are never spared. They are very eager for knowledge; and very fond of hearing about the things of God, chiefly when they do understand them. Most of them believe in the 'Men of Old', persons who lived like philosophers. Many of them worship the Sun and others the Moon. They like to hear things explained according to Reason; and granted that there are sins and vices among them, when one reasons with them, pointing out that what they do is evil, they are convinced by this reasoning.

Xavier preached in the streets and markets as he had done in Goa. But as before, the difficulties of making himself understood held him back. A Japanese who heard him, describes, 'a man tall of body, a gentleman, who did not understand the Japanese tongue, but preached through an interpreter and when he preached his face became red and inflamed.'

Xavier quickly realised that the Japanese were a civilised people with complicated beliefs of their own. So Christian priests in Japan had to learn the language and customs of the Japanese and not treat them as ignorant savages. The Jesuit priests who followed Xavier were careful to study the Japanese way of life and wrote enthusiastic letters home to Europe. Jesuits wrote reports from their missions all over the world, but the Japanese letters were some of the most interesting to their European readers. They were often so full of admiration for the Japanese that they had to be cut by their editors in Rome before they could be published. For the Church wanted the letters to show how necessary it was to save the heathen from their wicked ways and not to praise them!

Fr. Luis Frois came to Japan in 1563 after working in Goa for many years, and travelled straight to the capital, Miyako, now called Kyoto. Here he lived for eleven years learning to speak Japanese fluently and writing reports to Europe. Here are some of the things he wrote after he had arrived in Miyako on February 19, 1565:

About 400 years ago, all Japan was subject to one Emperor. But the nobles, rebelling against him, have taken away the greatest part of his kingdom, although his royal title remains and they pay great respect to him still. Thus the Empire of Japan is now divided into 66 kingdoms, the cause of civil war continually in the islands, while the kings invade one another, each one longing to make his kingdom greater. In the city of Miyako is the place of the Emperor whom the nation honours as a God. He has in his house 366 idols, one of which is set every night by his bedside to act as watchman. He is thought to be so holy that he is not allowed to walk on the ground.

As for the state of the country, the summers are most hot and the winters extremely cold. In the northern island [Hokkaido] there falls so much snow that the houses being buried in it, the inhabitants keep indoors certain months of the year, having no way to come out unless they break up the roof-tiles. Whirlwinds most strong, earthquakes so common that the Japanese have little or no fear of such things. The air is healthy, the waters good, the people very fair and well-built. They commonly go bare-headed, 85 rooting up with pincers all the hair of their heads as it grows, except a little piece behind which they knot and keep with great care. Even children wear daggers and swords, which they lay under their pillows when they go to bed. Their usual food is rice and salads and, near the seaside, fish. They feast one another many times and at these feasts take care that they do not rudely commit some fault and read certain books containing rules for ceremonies proper to banquets. In order to be well-behaved they put their food into their mouths with little sticks, counting it a great rudeness to touch it with their fingers. Winter and summer they drink water as hot as they can bear it. Their houses are finely-made and clean, laid all over with straw mats on which they both sit (instead of stools) and lie down in their clothes with wooden blocks under their heads as pillows. For fear of dirtying these mats, they either go barefoot indoors or wear straw leggings when they go abroad which they take off when they come home. Gentlemen spend the night in banqueting, music and idle talk, they sleep in the day time. In bringing up their children they only use words to correct them, using as much care and trouble with boys of six and seven as though they were old men. They are very fond of entertaining strangers of whom they love to ask with great curiosity even about trifles, what foreign nations do and their fashions.

(In this the Japanese were very different from the Chinese who never showed the slightest curiosity about their European visitors).

By 1550 the King of Portugal had taken control of the trade with Japan. He already appointed the men who were to captain the other voyages, to Goa, Malacca and China every year. The Portuguese now had control of almost all trade in the East, so these captains all became extremely rich. Many men were

Opposite: *A picture from a Dutch atlas of 1670 showing the palace of Yedo where the Emperor lived. It was the first to be visited by English travellers*

eager for the posts and the King used to reward those who had already done good service in the empire by giving the posts to them. The Japan voyage was added to the list of places to trade. Ralph Fitch described what he heard of it in 1585:

> When the Portuguese go from Macao in China to Japan, they carry much white silk, gold, musk and porcelain: and they bring from thence nothing but silver. They have a great carrack that goes there every year and she brings every year over 600,000 crusadoes of silver. And all this Japanese silver and 200,000 crusadoes more in silver which they bring every year from India, they spend with great profit in China.

The trade was profitable and the Jesuits in Japan received both a share in the profits and an increase in the numbers of Japanese who became Christians. In 1580, a Jesuit writer described this strange connection between the success of their mission and the Great Ship from Macao, the carrack, which the Japanese called the 'Black Ship' or 'Kurofune':

> Your Reverence must understand that after the Grace and Favour of God, the greatest help to us in converting Christians is that of the Great Ship. For, as the lords of Japan are very poor and the benefits they receive when the ships come into their ports are very great they try hard to persuade them to visit their cities. And as the Japanese know that the ships will only come to the places where there are Christians and churches many of them go to seek out priests to come there to set up churches. And as the Japanese are very obedient to their lords they readily become Christians when told to do so by their masters.

Xavier himself had made plans for a storehouse and market to be set up 'to the great benefit of the royal revenue of Portugal', and to provide some money every year for the Jesuit missionaries working in Japan. For, as another Jesuit writer said, 'If there were not merchants who go to seek for earthly treasure in the east and west Indies, who would transport there the preachers who take heavenly treasure?'

Ships of the Dutch East India Company setting sail for the East (about 1650)

Just as Prince Henry the Navigator had sent out his men to look for Christians and spices fifty years earlier, the Portuguese were still as anxious to convert the heathen as to make profits. The other nations, England and Holland, who had joined the Portuguese in the Indian Ocean were interested only in trade. In the later part of the sixteenth century they took a larger and larger share of Portugal's markets. Her empire began to decline, although she kept her colonies in Goa and the east coast of Africa until the middle of the twentieth century. As Portugal grew weaker, England and Holland began to compete with each other for the largest share of the eastern trade. In 1599 the Dutch, encouraged by the publication by Jan van Linschoten of his books and maps, set up their East India Company to provide the money for regular trading expeditions to the Indies. In 1601, the English founded their East India Company and Richard Hakluyt was a founder-member. From that time the two Companies became the chief rivals for the eastern trade round the Cape of Good Hope.

How Do We Know?

You will remember that many of the early accounts of Portuguese sailors were kept secret for fear that other nations would find the way to their new markets in the East. They did keep very detailed records, charts, maps and notebooks called 'Roteiros' in which every step of a particular voyage was given so that other ships would know exactly how to steer into harbour or where there were hidden reefs. These were all filed away in the offices of the Royal Library in Lisbon and many of them have only been published for the first time in the last hundred years. As news spread of the new eastern routes people became curious, and in other countries in Europe booksellers and scholars began to collect traveller's tales which became very popular. In England, Richard Hakluyt, a 'Scholar of the University of Oxford', published one of the most famous of these collections, called, 'The Principall Navigations, Voyages, Traffique and Discoveries of the English Nation, made by Sea or Overland, to the Remote and Farthest Distant Quarters of the Earth at any time within the Compasse of these 1600 Yeares.'

As you will see from his title, Hakluyt was particularly interested in English discoveries. But this did not stop him printing accounts from abroad, even by his rival, Jan van Linschoten in Holland, if he felt that they would help to persuade the English merchants and seamen to take a larger part in the eastern trade. As you know, he was to be one of the founders of the East India Company in 1601 which put up the money to buy cargoes and equip ships for the East. This Company was to become so powerful in India that by the middle of the eighteenth century it acted almost like part of the British government.

Hakluyt's collection of travels, which I have often quoted in this book, was continued shortly afterwards by Samuel Purchas in his even larger collection called 'Hakluytus Posthumous' (or 'A Continuation of Hakluyt') but better known by the later part of its title, 'Purchas His Pilgrims', published in 1621. Hakluyt and Purchas were able to include a few of the Portuguese accounts but Hakluyt also used the accounts of seamen he met himself in London. He persuaded Ralph Fitch, for example, to write down accounts of his adventures so that they could be published in his book. By Purchas' day, more of the accounts of early Portuguese travels had been published in Europe. He collected some of them and that is why I have used his accounts of the explorations made for Henry the Navigator and for the voyages of Vasco da Gama.

Some of the most interesting writers of this period were not included in either Hakluyt's or Purchas' travels. They can be found in the volumes published by the Hakluyt Society, translated into English from the Spanish or Portuguese or Italian in which they were written. In these volumes you will find the Journals of the Italian, Cadamosto, and the letters of the great Portuguese Viceroy Affonso d'Albuquerque, as well as the complete journal of Peter Mundy, the English sailor.

You will also remember that from the time when the first Jesuit missionary, St. Francis Xavier, began his work in the East, letters and reports were constantly sent back to Europe by Jesuit missions abroad. They began to be published regularly in the form of letter-books and became very popular. They do not always report fairly what they saw, for the missionaries were naturally unable to approve of the strange new religions they met in the East. But they were the first accounts of India, China and Japan to reach Europe from men who were highly educated, not simple seamen like Ralph Fitch and Peter Mundy.

Things To Do

1. If you followed Pegolotti's route to China today, which countries would you go through and in what different ways could you travel?
2. How is silk made? If you can, rear some silkworms yourself.
3. Make a 'lead' and take soundings to find out the depth of a pool. Can you make a chart of the bottom?
4. Find samples of as many spices as you can, describe how they grow, and show where they come from on a map.
5. Describe a voyage from the Cape of Good Hope to Macao. Where would you stop on the way and what would you see?
6. What can you find out about the religions of India or China when the Portuguese arrived there?
7. What sort of things did Moghul emperors or Japanese gentlemen enjoy? Which would you prefer to be?
8. Things to draw—the Emperor Prester John; the court of the King of Calicut; Gentlemen of Goa out for a walk; English pirates attacking a Portuguese ship; the Taj Mahal; the white elephants of Pegu having a bath; the Great Ship arriving in Japan.
9. Imagine you are with St. Francis Xavier preaching in India or Japan. What do people ask him and what does he reply?
10. Imagine you are sailing into a strange harbour for the first time. Make a 'Roteiro' or route-map so that other ships can follow your route safely.
11. Scurvy was a terrible disease. Find out how Captain Cook saved his sailors from it on his voyage to Australia.

Glossary

archipelago, the name for a collection of islands

bazaar, oriental market, sometimes covered over to keep out the sun

bosun's pipe, the bosun (short for boatswain) would signal the different watches on the ship or give the orders for some fresh task by blowing a small pipe or whistle, rather like the signals given on a bugle in the army

Byzantine, of Byzantium which was the old name for Constantinople (Istanbul)

camphor, white crystals with a strong smell used in drugs and to store goods and clothes as it keeps insects away

carat, a measure of the purity of gold. The purest gold is 24 carats

caravel, small light ship chiefly built in Spain and Portugal and only in use in the fifteenth to seventeenth centuries

caulker, craftsman who stopped the seams, or gaps between the planks of wooden ships, with oakum (a kind of rope-like material) and melted pitch, to prevent the water coming in

chestnuts, these are the water-chestnuts found in Chinese food, not chestnuts grown on trees. They come from the roots of a water plant

convert, someone who changes his religion

crusados, a Portuguese coin with the figure of the cross on it, now worth about ten pence

factories, at this time this was the name for a company's trading stations overseas, where it kept its equipment and goods

fast days, days on which the Church said people must eat less and eat no meat

Great Pound/Little Pound, at this time different cities had different weights and measures. The Little Pound was the pound of Genoa in Italy, and the Great Pound was worth thirty Little Pounds. It may have been a local Russian weight

Hindu, believer in Hinduism, the most ancient religion of India, in which several gods and goddesses are worshipped. Hindus are divided into different classes, or 'castes' and Hinduism still has more followers than any other religion in India today

ingot, solid block of cast metal, usually steel, silver or gold

junk, large Chinese ship used either as a warship or to carry cargo. Junks were wide-based so that they could ride the typhoons of the East China Seas and could carry as much cargo as the biggest European ships at this time. The first European sailors to the east were amazed at their size

lateen sails, a triangular sail set at an angle of 45° from the mast on a long yard-arm. Used on Arab ships in the Indian ocean as well as on Portuguese, lateen sails were copied from Moorish ships on the North African coast

lead, a lump of lead let down on a rope from a ship to find out how deep the water is

litter, couch with curtains round it carried on the shoulders of servants by long poles, in which important people were carried about in India and the Far East

madder, plant with yellow flowers whose roots provide a red dye

mandarin, Chinese official, something like our magistrates or ministers, who was appointed by the Emperor to work in his Civil Service and govern a city or a province

mariners' compass, the north-pointing magnetic compass

monsoons, winds in the Indian ocean and S.E. Asia which blow from the N.E. in winter bringing dry weather and from the S.W. in summer, bringing rain

Moors, the Moslem peoples who lived in North Africa. They were for several centuries the rulers of Spain and Portugal as well

Moslem, one who is a believer in the faith called 'Islam'. There is one God, Allah, and Mohammed is His prophet, who revealed the laws of God to men. These laws are preserved in the holy book called the Koran

musk, a substance obtained from the male musk-deer which was used in the making of perfumes

nomad, wandering tribesman

pagan, this term was used by the people of the Elizabethan period to refer to nations who were not Christian, but chiefly those who were believers in rather primitive faiths and not usually those who were Moslems or Hindus

pinnace, a small ship, usually with double banks of oars, rather than sails. Used to accompany larger ships on long voyages, rather like a ship's boat

porcelain, very hard, fine china first produced in China and very highly prized in Europe. The secret of making porcelain was not discovered in the west until the eighteenth century

scourge, this means a whip, and so someone who is thought of as being sent to punish others

scurvy, a painful disease which sailors suffered when they had no fresh fruit or vegetables for a long time. It is caused by a lack of vitamin C

square-rigged, where the chief sails are set at right angles to the length of the ship and hung from the mast on horizontal poles or 'yards'

sulphur/brimstone, these are the same thing, a yellow chemical used in the making of gunpowder

tributary, China thought of most foreign states as 'tributary', that is subject to her and bringing her tribute

typhoon, a violent storm of wind in south-east Asia and the China Sea

Index